OUTLINE GRAMMAR

OF

THE LHOTA NAGA LANGUAGE;

WITH

A VOCABULARY AND ILLUSTRATIVE SENTENCES

OUTLINE GRAMMAR

OF

THE LHOTA NAGA LANGUAGE;

WITH

A VOCABULARY AND ILLUSTRATIVE SENTENCES

W. E. WITTER

GYAN

Published by

Gyan Publishing House
5, Ansari Road
Daryaganj, New Delhi-110002
Phone: 011-47034999, 9811692060
E-mail: books@gyanbooks.com

Distribution Network
gyanbooks.com
India, USA, Canada, UK, Australia

ISBN: 978-93-6780-049-2 (HB)

First Published, 1888

2nd Impression 2024

Printed at: Gyan Press, Delhi.

OUTLINE GRAMMAR OF THE LHOTA NAGA LANGUAGE
Author: W. E. WITTER

OUTLINE GRAMMAR

OF

THE LHŌTĀ NĀGĀ LANGUAGE;

WITH

A VOCABULARY AND ILLUSTRATIVE SENTENCES.

BY

REV. W. E. WITTER, M.A.,
WOKHA, NAGA HILLS, ASSAM.

CALCUTTA:
PRINTED BY THE SUPERINTENDENT OF GOVERNMENT PRINTING, INDIA.
1888.

TABLE OF CONTENTS.

PREFACE.

My object in preparing this brief work has been to furnish some assistance to any who, either in the interests of good government or of the Christian religion, may wish to acquire the Lhōta Nāgā language.

With the exception of a few words collected by Captain John Butler, B.S.C., the following Outline Grammar, with a vocabulary and illustrative sentences, is the first presentation of the speech of the Lhōta Nāgās.

I gratefully acknowledge the interest taken in my labours by Mr. W. E. Ward, M.A., C.S., Chief Commissioner of Assam, through whose kindness this publication has been made possible; and also the assistance I have derived from the perusal of an article by Mr. John Avery, M.A., on the "Aō Nāgā Language of Southern Assam," reprinted from the American Journal of Philology, Volume VII, No. 3, and an "Outline Grammar of the Angami Nāgā Language" by Mr. R. B. McCabe, C.S.

I am especially indebted to my wife, who has travelled with me through the mazes of this new language and by many helpful suggestions has added much to the accuracy of the following pages.

W. E. WITTER.

WOKHA NAGA HILLS,
The 9th September 1887.

ALPHABET.

In preparing the following pages for the Government Press, I have followed the suggestions of Mr. C. J. Lyall, C.I.E., employing as an alphabet for the Lhōtā Nāgā language the Roman character with the help of diacritical marks, as follows :—

VOWELS.

a—unmarked, short as in "company," like the sound of *u* in "but."

ā—long, as in "father."

å—broad, as in "ball."

à—sharp, as in "pan."

e—unmarked, as in "then," "met," "bed."

é—for the sound of *ey* in "they" or *ai* in "aim."

i—unmarked, as in "thin."

ī—long, as in "machine," never for *i* in "shine."

o—unmarked, a medium sound, neither so short as in "not" nor so long as in "naught."

ō—long, as in "bone."

ö—a peculiar sound, somewhat resembling the German *ö* in "schön."

u—like *u* in "pull," "bull," never the sound of *u* in "hull," "skull."

ū—long sound of *oo* in English.

ü—a thin, light sound of *u*, about half-way between the sound of *u* in "but" and the sound of *u* in "bull."

DIPHTHONGS.

ai—as *ie* in "lie."

au—as *ow* in "how."

yū—as *ui* in "suit."

oi—as *oy* in "boy."

CONSONANTS.

b—as in English.

c—is discarded, except in *ch* as in "church," and *chh* a prolongation of the same sound, and when it follows the letter *s* in order to prolong or slightly aspirate that letter.

d—as in English.

f—as in English.

g—discarded, except when in combination with *n*, as in "song."
j—discarded.
k—as in English.
l—as in English.
m—as in English.
n—as in "now."
ṇ—gives a nasal intonation to a vowel, and corresponds with the *sundrobindu* ̐ of Assamese and Bengali. This nasal intonation of vowels is very common in Lhōtā Nāgā.
ng—like *ng* in "song."
p—as in English.
q—discarded. *kw* = the sound of *qu* in "queer."
r—as in English.
rr—employed when *r* is strongly trilled.
s—as in "this."
sh—as in "shall."
t—as in English.
th—as in "hot-house."
v—as in English.
w—as in English.
x—discarded.
z—as in English.

Lhōtā Nāgā unlike the *Aō* abounds in aspirate consonants. Besides those above mentioned, the following are more or less frequent:—

dh, *fh*, *kh*, *lh*, *mh*, *ph*, *phh*, *rh* and *zh*.

A peculiar sound is sometimes given to the consonants *d* and *l*. As these sounds are infrequent and can only be learned by ear, I have thought it unnecessary to add any distinguishing mark.

The letters *b*, *k* and *v* are often mute, as is also *g* following *n*.

The number of letters that are used interchangeably in Lhōtā Nāgā are surprisingly large: some are interchangeable in certain words, and not in others.

A few illustrations will indicate the variety of these mutations.

Vowels.

a and *ā*—lamatero, lamātero = this and that.
ā and *e*—tāro, tero = ten.
ā and *o*—nnā, nno = you.
å and *o*—rokrå, rōkro = sixty.
e and *i*—thenī, thingī = with, toward.
e and *ī*—mepōk, mīpōk = ashes.

e and *ai*—yāntse, yāntsai = poor man.
ī and *ü*—otsī, otsü = rice.
ō and *ü*—nchōkāpeṉ, nchükāpeṉ = daily.
ö and *yū*—ōchö, ōchyū = tomorrow.
üe and *wi*—efüe, efwī = thief.

CONSONANTS.

b and *p*—ōlab, ōkap = a grave.
b and *v*—ekab, ekav = a bribe.
ch and *kh*—ōkhīā, ōchīā = who.
dl and *dr*—ekō hendlyūwo, ekō hendrūwo = a span.
h and *p*—tāmhō, tāmpō = another.
kh and *th*—khīālā, thīālā = shoots.
l and *n*—n-lī, n-nī = is not.
m and *p*—ōmōmō, ōpōpō = himself.
m and *n*—m-mā, n-vā = is not.
m and *v*—m-mā, n-vā = is not.
m and *w*—m-mo, n-wo = not go.
n and *y*—nī, yī = you.
n and *ṉ*—ōlān, ōlāṉ = road, path.
n and *ng*—thenī, thingī = with, to.
p and *s*—pōkthetā, sokthetā = put on the upper cloth.
tsü and *tzü*—kyōṉtsü, kyōṉtzü = all men.

OUTLINE GRAMMAR

OF

THE LHŌTĀ NĀGĀ LANGUAGE,

WITH

A VOCABULARY AND ILLUSTRATIVE SENTENCES.

Lhōtā Nāgā may be described as a "non-Aryan" language of the Indo-Chinese stock.

It constitutes the speech of about thirty thousand Nāgās who occupy sixty villages, all but four of which are included in the Wokha subdivision of the Nāgā hills.

Their location may be more exactly defined as lying on the southern edge of the Sibsagar district, having as their southern boundary the Doyang river as it enters the hills, and thence following the curve of the hills to about 20° 20′ N. Lat., where they are met by the Aō or Hatigōriā tribe of Nāgās.

Like the speech of neighbouring tribes, Lhōtā Nāgā is found to be in the early stages of agglutination.

Its monosyllabic base is quite apparent, but in its present state it is unquestionably rather dissyllabic than monosyllabic. In this it corresponds with Aō Nāgā.

The tendency to dissyllabify the language is seen from the fact that nearly every noun, which would otherwise be a monosyllable, becomes a dissyllable by assuming the prefix *ō*, which prefix is again dropped so soon as a possessive or modifying word can unite with the stem of the noun to form a dissyllable, *e.g.*,—

Ōyāṉ = village.
Ṉiyāṉ = your village.
Otchhü = water.
Elam = hot.
Tchülam = hot-water.

Pronunciation.

The marked varieties of intonation and pronunciation of words and sentences among persons of the same, and more particularly among those of different villages, together with the use of certain root words, which, in the development of the language, have lapsed into so vague and general a signification, that they are now simply used as particles to modify the meaning, and relations of other words constitute the chief difficulties in acquiring the languages of these rude hill tribes.

The chief cause of the difference in the pronunciation of words is clearly traceable to the isolated lives of the natives. As each village occupies a separate hill-top and has little communication with other villages, except for occasional purposes of trade, or when they join the war-path against some common enemy, a dialect is developed, distinguishable at once from that of every other village.

Again, in all Nāgā land there are small groups of villages which, by frequent and friendly intercourse, have produced dialects characteristic of these several groups.

In acquiring the language it is well to employ, as far as possible, individuals representing these several groups, especially if the difference in dialects is not too marked.

Lhōtā Nāgā has been very aptly characterised as a "hilly language." Sentences are sometimes spoken in waves of sound, beautifully balanced, and not unmusical. More often, however, the progress of a sentence is jagged, abrupt and precipitous in its utterance. Slight difference in stress is the only distinguishing feature of many words. Thus, *yiā* means either to go or to come, *ōyān* = a village or another person, *ōsā* = a sitting-place or to wait, *ōnūng* = pith or a stone, &c., &c.

These differences in accent can only be properly learned by ear, and I have made no attempt to mark tones or emphasis except in the single instance of negatives. These are indicated by a dash following the syllable of negation, which is always to be pronounced on a much higher key than the rest of the word.

M-mā = is not.

Mmā = stomach. (The two ems in the latter case are to be pronounced on nearly the same key.)

N-lī = is not.
Nlī, or *nnī* = tongue.

It should also be remembered that the voice always falls at the close of a sentence, and in double interrogatives, where the verbal root is reduplicated, the first syllable of the interrogative verb is to be spoken on a much higher key than the rest of the word. These forms of interrogation are fully explained under interrogative forms of the verb.

For remarks on interchangeable and mute letters, see under Alphabet.

In the study of Lhōtā Nāgā much care should be taken to ascertain, so far as possible, the precise meaning in each case of those root-words which have ceased to be used as words by themselves, but combine with the roots of other words to modify their meanings and relations.—*See* under Verbal Modifiers.

ARTICLE.

Indefinite Article.—In Lhōtā Nāgā the place of the indefinite article is supplied by the demonstrative particles *nchyūā* = "one," referring to individuals of the human species, and *matsangā* or *ntsangā* = "one" of any class of objects.

I see a man—
Ānā Kyōṉ nchyūā hüngālā.
" " *matsangā* "
Lit.—I man one see.

I see a bird—
Ānā wōro matsangā hüngālā.
" " *ntsangā* "
Lit.—I bird one see.

The above particles are employed, however, only when special attention is drawn to the fact that but one object is mentioned.

Definite Article.—Strictly speaking, there is no definite article. Its place is supplied by the demonstrative pronouns *shi* = "this" and *chi* = "that," and by the relative pronoun *chi* or *chü* = "the one."

Give me the book.
Kāko shi ā piā.
Lit.—Book this me give.

Give me the walking-stick.
Chārōng chī ā piā.
Lit.—Walking-stick that (at some distance) me give.

The boy who came yesterday.
Nchö nūngôr erōwōchi.
Lit.—Yesterday boy coming the one.

The particle *cho* also, a frequent affix of nouns and pronouns, seems often to have the force of the definite article :

This is good, that is bad.

Shicho mhōnā, ōchicho m-mho.

Lit.—This the good, that the bad.

NOUNS.

I.—Classification.

Under the classification of nouns I need only refer to the formation of collective, verbal or participial, and diminutive nouns.

I.—Collective nouns are formed by affixes or added words signifying a collection of objects of the same kind :—

The affix *tzü* or *tsü* signifies all, large, whole.

Kyōṉtzü = all men.

Metātzü = all places, the whole place.

Yāntzü = a large village, — one containing many men and many houses.

Kyōṉtzüyāṉ = all villages.

Oyaṉ ekāni = the whole village, — all the inhabitants, all the fighting men.

The affix *yo* from *ōyo* = a group, clump.

Kyōṉyo = a group of men.

Ōtōngyo = a clump of trees.

Eyo = we (the group of us).

The affix *teṉ* from *oteṉ* = herd, flock, shoal.

Māngsüteṉ = a herd of cows.

Nteṉ = you (several), (the flock of you).

Wōroteṉ = a flock of birds.

Ongoteṉ = a shoal of fish.

II.—Verbal or participial nouns are formed by—

(1) Affixing *pheṉ* or *peṉ* to the verbal root :—

Kōkthe = to sit.

Kōkthepheṉ = a sitting-place, a chair.

Erām = to write.

Erāmpheṉ = an instrument for writing, a pen.

(2) By affixing *eṉ* to the verbal root :—

Shisho = to trade.

Shishoeṉ = a trader.

Ōyōncho = to work in metals.

Ōyōnchōen̲ = a worker in metals, a blacksmith.
Yōnchōen̲ = " " " "

(3) By employing both the prefix *e* and the affix *en̲* :—
Ōyōncho = to work in metals.
Ōyōn̲ echoen̲ = a worker in metals.
Vü = to sew.
Evüen̲ = a tailor.

When the verbal root ends in *ān* or *en*, the derivative noun is formed by simply changing the final *n* to *n̲* nasal, and prefixing *e* to the verbal root. The prefix *e* is sometimes suppressed for the sake of euphony :—

Ōngoyen = to sell fish.	*Erān* = to write.
Ōngoeyen̲ = a fish-monger.	*Erān̲* = a writer.

4. By affixing to the verbal root the participial affix *wō*, sometimes for euphony *mō* or *ō*, one form of the verb "to go" signifying "gone," "become", and the further affix *chī*, the third personal pronoun, which, when thus employed, becomes a relative. Nouns thus formed generally take the prefix *e :*

Tso = to eat.	*Vān* = to stay.
Etsōwōchi = (he) who eats.	*Evān̲mōchi* = the one who stays.

See again under formation of adjectives.
Diminutive nouns are formed by means of the affixes *ro*, *dro*, *rōro*—

Village = *Ōyān.*	Duck = *Photak.*
Small village = *Yāndro.*	Duckling = *Photakro.*
Leaf = *Lōmo.*	Woman = *Elüē.*
Leaflet = *Lōmōro.*	Girl = *Elüērōro.*

NOTE 1.—The affix *pōe* used with nouns signifies "another" :

Yāmpōe = another village.
Nzüpōe = another year.
Tsangpōe } = another day.
Engipōe }

NOTE 2.—The word *thāmpo, thāmho,* signifying another, sometimes becomes an affix, and itself takes the affix *thang* denoting "time":

Ōyān = village.
Yānthamo = another village.
Tāmpōthang } = another time.
Tāmhōthang }

NOTE 3.—Nearly every noun which is not a dissyllable becomes such by means of the prefix *ō*, which is again dropped so soon as a possessive or other modifying word can unite with it to form a word of two or more syllables :

Ōki = house.	*Shenā* = hot.
Āki = my house.	*Tchhüshen* = hot-water.
Otchhü = water.	*Ōtōng* = tree.
Elamo = hot.	*Etsi* = Sahab.
Tchhülam = hot-water.	*Etsitōng* = Sahab's tree.

ATTRIBUTES OF NOUNS.

I.—Gender.

In Lhōtā Nāgā the distinctions of gender apply only to animate objects, which are either male or female, and are indicated in two ways:—

(1) By the use of different sexual names which are confined to words implying human relationships.

(2) By added words for male and female.

I.—Different Sexual Names.

Masculine.	Feminine.
Bachelor = *Khyandrōe.*	Maid = *Lōroe.*
Boy = *Ōngo.*	Girl = *Ōkā.*
Brother (younger) = *Ōnyūi*	Sister = *Ōyūlüe.*
(older) = *Ōtā.*	
Brother-in-law = *Ōnāng.*	Sister-in-law = *Omī.*
Father = *Ōpō.*	Mother = *Ōyo, ōpvu.*
Grandfather = *Ōmotsü.*	Grandmother = *Ōtsü.*
Husband = *Ōrāpvü.*	Wife = *E-ng.*
Husband = *Ōki khamo.*	Wife = *Ōki kham.*
Uncle (paternal) *Ōpōramo, Ōpōrō.*	Aunt (paternal) = *Ōno.*
Uncle (maternal) *Ōmo.*	Aunt (maternal) = *Ōphyo.*

II.—Added words for Male and Female.

These words differ somewhat according to the class of objects referred to. Thus, the word for male is *epüē*, and the word for female *elüē*, respectively, of human beings, and *ōpōng* = male, and *ōkhö* = female, when applied to the lower animals.

(*1*) *Added words for Male and Female:—Human Species.*

As in other languages, many names of animate objects convey in themselves no idea of gender:

Nūngōr = any young person, not an adult.

Nūngōr epüē = boy; *Nūngōr elüē* = girl.

Ōtsōe = child.

Ōtsōe epüē = male child; *Ōtsōe elüē* = female child.

Ngāro = infant.

Ngāro epüē = male infant.
Ngāro elüē = female infant.

Chenchi engai = servant.

Chenchi engai epüē = man servant. *Chenchi engai elüē* = female servant.

Kyōn̲ = a Lhōtā Nāgā.

Kyōn̲ epüē = a Lhōtā man. *Kyōn̲ elüē* = a Lhōtā woman, *Nāgini*.

The word *kyōn̲* seems to be the nearest approach to a general term for man, although in its general application it has reference only to individuals of the Lhōtā tribe.

(2) *Added words for Male and Female:—Lower Animals.*

Phurro = dog.

Masc.—Phurro ōpōng, phurro pōng, phupōng.
Fem.—Phurro ōkhö.

Ziro = rat.

Masc.—Ziro ōpōng, ziro pōng.
Fem.—Ziro ōkhö.

Hōno = fowl.

Masc.—Hāmpōng = cock.
Fem.—Hānkhö = hen.

NOTE.—It will be seen from the above that these added words by contraction often become really affixes of the term denoting the species. Sometimes, owing to euphonic changes, quite a different word is produced. Thus, the words for cock and hen noted above.

II.—NUMBER.

In Lhōtā, as in other Nāgā languages, number is indicated by no special sign when the context renders this unnecessary.

When, however, the context is considered an insufficient guide as to the number of objects referred to, *nchūā* = "one," applied only to individuals of the human species, and *matsangā* or *ntsangā* = "one" of any class of objects, are used to denote the singular number; and either the demonstrative pronouns *shiāng, shiāno, hiāno* = "these," and *chiāng*, *chiāno*, *chiān̠*, *ọteno* = "those," or one of several nouns of multitude, are used to denote plurality of objects:

Yesterday a man came.
Nchö kyōn nchyūā rōcho.

Lit.—Yesterday man one came.

Nchö nchyūā rōā.

Lit.—Yesterday one (man) came.

I have one horse.
A korr matsangā liā.

Lit.—My horse one is.

The men have gone.
Kyōn̠ shiāng yichākā.
Kyōn̠ chiāng yichākā.
Kyōn̠ ōtēnā yichākā.

The more common nouns of multitude are *ōten* = flock, herd, shoal; *ōyo* = a clump, group; *khōlōk* = a pile, a company, a gathering; *enni etham* = two or three; *mezü mūngo* = four or five, &c., &c., signify "several."

Terrāro = a few, several.
Elam = many.

In Lhōtā, as in the Aō and Angāmī Nāgā languages, a rudimentary dual is seen in the use of the numeral adjective two = *ōnī* in Lhōtā (*nā* in Aō and Angamī) whenever they wish to express duality.

He and my brother have gone to the bazaar.
Shihā ātā ōni shī shọpheni īyā.

Lit.—He and my brother two bazaar to have gone.

We (he and I) will come.
Shī enī iyū.

Lit.—He we two will come.

NOTE.—Angāmī Nāgā for the same would be *He nā vōrtōwe.*

Andrew and Philip.
Andriā Filip ōni.

Lit.—Andrew Philip two.

NOTE.—*Aō Nāgā* for the above would be *Andriā āser Filip nā.*
Lit.—Andrew and Philip two.

In Lhōtā the word for two is occasionally omitted when two are spoken of:

My brother and his brother went.
Atā nā shi ōtā tō wōcho.

Here the particle *nā* is the conjunction "and," and the particle *tō* following *ōtā* is frequently used when two or more objects are spoken of in succession.

III.—Case.

In Lhōtā Nāgā case relations are denoted by an incomplete system of declension, and also by the use of postpositions—words used like prepositions but always placed after the word governed.

1.—Nominative Case.

(1) The subject-nominative of an active transitive verb ends in *nā*.

When there are two or more nominatives to the same verb, the particle *nā* is affixed only to the one nearest the verb.

The conjunction *nā* = "and" is not to be confounded with the affix *nā* of the subject-nominative.

(2) The subject-nominative of an intransitive verb is generally the crude form of the noun, or the crude form with the affix *cho*. Occasionally, however, the subject of an intransitive verb ends in *nā*.

The horse eats grass.
Korrnā ōchāk tsōālā.

Your father is calling you.
Nipōnā ni tsālā.

Your brother and my brother killed a tiger.
Nitā nā ātātōnā mhurr langtātā.

Note.—The *nā* following *nitā* is the conjunction "and," and the *nā* affixed to *ātātō* the sign of the nominative case.

This is good, but that is bad.
Hicho mhōnā, ōsi ōchicho m-mhō.

I am tired.
Á mōktātā.

The cow is hungry.
Māngsü wōntōntsangā.
,, wōntōntātā.

I will go.
Ānā wō, aiyo wō.

He has gone.
Shi yichakā, shinā yichākā.

2.—*Genitive Case.*

The genitive case is expressed simply by position before the governing noun:

What is your brother's name?
Nitā myangcho ōchōwēlā?
Lit.—Your brother name what is?

His name is Ōnhyūwo.
Shī myang Ōnhyūwo.
Shī myangcho Ōnhyūwo.

3.—*Dative Case.*

Nouns in the dative end in *i* = "to" and *o* = "for," or take the postpositions *etchī, etchü, etscōnā* = "for," *theni, thingi* = "to," and *pānā, nzo, sirrā* and *theni, thingi* = "with." These last may be classed as dative or ablative of accompaniment:

I will go to your village.
Ānā ni yāni wo.
Lit.—I your village to will go.

NOTE.—When the noun ends in *ā*, it unites with the *i*, the sign of the dative, to form the diphthong *ai*: *e.g.*—

I will go to the jungle.
Ānā ōrai wō.

He has gone for wood.
Shīnā ōtsango iyā.

I came to see your house.
Ānā niki zelo rōcho.
Lit.—I your house for (the purpose of) seeing came.

Sometimes the noun remains unchanged:

Give this to Onhyuwo.
Shi Ōnhyūwo piā.

The dative "for" expressed by means of the postposition *etchü*, *etchi* or *etscōnā*:

Buy a cloth for my brother.
Ā tā etchü ōscü shiā.
Lit.—My brother for cloth buy.

When persons are spoken of in the dative case with "to," this preposition is sometimes indicated by the postposition *theni* or *thingi*: *e.g.*—

Go to the Sahab.
Etsi theni wōā.

The Babu sold his pony to my brother.
Bābūnā ōmō korr ātā theni yenā.

The following sentences illustrate the use of the dative or ablative of accompaniment:—

He eats with me.
Shinā ā theni ōtsi tsōālā.

Come with me.
Ā pānā rōā.

He went with the Sahab.
Shicho etsi sirrā wōcho.

He stays with me.
Shinā ā nzo vānālā.

We sleep together
Eni nzo yipālā.

It will be seen in the last two sentences that *nzo* seems to be used in the one case as a postposition governing the pronoun *ā*, and, in the other case, as an adverb of manner qualifying the verb.

4.—Accusative Case.

In the accusative case we have the crude form of the noun: *e.g.*—

He eats salt = *Shinā ōmā tsōālā.*

When the verb has two objective complements, one direct and the other indirect, the latter stands nearest the verb: *e.g.*—

He gave me salt = *Shinā ōmā ā picho.*

5.—Ablative Case.

The affix *nā* is generally the sign of the ablative case. It is, however, sometimes omitted: *e.g.*—

Whence did you come?
Nno kūinā rōchōlā?

I came from my house.
Ā kinā rōcho.

He has gone from here.
Shi hellōnā yichākā.

I killed him with (by means of) a stone.
Ānā ōnungnā shi ephiātsangcho.

You go by boat, I'll go afoot.
Nno ōhrōngenā wōā, aiyo ōchōenā iyū.

For postpositions see under Dative and Locative Cases.

6.—*Locative Case.*

In the locative case we have the crude form of the noun, the same with the terminations *i* = "in," *o* or *lo* = "on," and *we* or *wi* = "in the direction of," "on," "upon," or the simple noun with the postpositions:—

Ōnūngi = in, among.
Tāchüngī = in, inside.
Ōpōni = on, upon.
Ōkapī= below, under, &c., &c.

Put this in the basket = { *Shīcho ōhai thetā.* / *Shīcho ōhā nūngī thetā.* }

The book is on the ground = { *Kāko lōko līa.* / *Kako lōkolo liā.* }

The fruit is on the tree = { *Tsangthī ōtōngo liā.* / *Tsangthī ōtōngwe mpāpā.* }

He is in the house = *Shī ōkī tāchüngı vānā.*

The orange is on the table = *Kōngken pīlang pōnī līā.*

Put my shoes under the table = *Ā chōkab pilang kapi vātā.*

You stand at my left hand and let him stand at my right hand = *Nno āmymwe vānā, shi aiyiwe vāntōkā.*

Still other postpositions will be found in the Vocabulary, in the list of Postpositions and in the list of Adverbs, Adverbial Phrases and Affixes.

NOTE 1.—Nouns and adverbs take the affix *tī*, *kī*, signifying "only," "alone," 'just," "only."

Only the Sahab came = *Etsiti rōcho.*
He has just gone = *Nthāngāti iyā.*

NOTE 2.—It will be found that the case endings and postpositions mentioned above interchange their meanings to some extent according to the words with which they happen to be used, as is also the case in *Aō Nāgā.*

NOTE 3.—When a noun is modified by a following adjective, the case temination or the postposition follows the latter, or, in other words, the adjective is inflected instead of the noun. This is also the case in *Āō Nāgā : e.g.*—

My white pony eats oranges—
Ā korr emmhüwochina kōngke tsōālā.

There is much fruit on the large tree.
Ōtōng tsapōlo tsangthī elam liā.

Lit.—Tree large on fruit much is.

The red hen is a great layer.
Hōno emyammochüna elam echiālā.

NOTE 4.—Nouns, adjectives and verbs are in their root forms indistinguishable from one another: *e.g.*—

Eatables = { *Etsōwo.* / *Tsōpeṅ epeṅ.* / *Etsōyü* (food and drink).

Eatable = *Etsōwo.*
Not eatable = *N-tsōwo.*
Good to eat = *Etsō mhōnā.*
An eater = *Etsōe, tsōe.*
The one who eats = *Etsōwōchi, etsōwochü.*
Eating = *Tsōna.*
Eats = *Tsoālā, tsōā, tsō.*
To eat = *Tsō, etsōlo, tsōlo.*

NOTE 5.—The particle *e*, which often appears as a prefix to nouns, adjectives and supines, seems like the prefix *te* before consonants and *t* before vowels in Aō Nāgā to have no formative significance, and may be assumed or thrown off at pleasure. It is perhaps slightly intensive in character, but is more likely assumed for the sake of euphony and to avoid the occurrence of monosyllabic words.

ADJECTIVES.

1.—FORMATION.

As noted above, adjectives take the case affixes of the nouns which they qualify, or are followed by the postpositions governing those nouns. In this sense only can they be said to have declension:—

There is fruit on the tall tree = *Ōtōng sapōlo tsangthi mpāpā.*
Lit.—Tree tall on fruit is.

My new pony kicked a boy = *Ā korr ethānā nüngōr epācho.*
Lit.—My pony new boy kicked.

Adjectives sometimes precede the nouns which they qualify:—
A wise man = *Ntsü kyōn.*

Simple adjectives are made participial or verbal by means of the double affix *wōchi*, explained under verbal or participial nouns. These participial adjectives have a prevailingly relative sense and stand in situations where in English we ordinarily employ a relative clause:—

Put the "dao" in the large basket = *Ōhān tsapōwōchi nüngi lepōk hi thetā.*

Lit.—Basket large the one in "dao" this place.

NOTE 1.—It is interesting to note that in Aō Nāgā the particle *bā* changed from *pā*, the third personal pronoun, becomes the affix of verbal adjectives and nouns, and is used in a relative sense precisely as *chī* or *chü* in Lhōtā.

Thus in Aō—

Bushi = sought.
Bushibā = (he) who sought.

In Lhōtā—

Yāna = seeking, sought.

Yāmmōchi = { seeking gone the one. (he) who seeks. (he) who sought. the seeker. }

NOTE 2.—Professor John Avery, in his Outline of "The Aō Nāgā in Southern Assam," says a suffix nearly identical in form and use with the one in Aō quoted above occurs in Lepcha, thus from *rōk* = "to read" is formed *rōbō* = "a reader."

In *Lhōtā*—

Erām = tc write.

Erāmmōchi = { writing gone the one (he) who writes, the writer. }

Professor Avery adds, "It is curious also to observe the syllable *bā* is both the relative pronoun and the adjective-forming prefix in Khasi, a language which, though bordering on the Nāgā tongues, is supposed to be quite unrelated to them."

NOTE 3.—The use of the participial affix *wō* = "gone," "become" in the formation of verbal or participial adjectives and nouns, may perhaps be more readily understood, if we illustrate some of its uses as a verb and participle :—

How old are you ?
Ni pōksi nzü kōtā wōlā ?
Lit.—You having been born years how many gone ?

How many days has he been absent ?
Shi yisi nchōk kōtā wōlā ?
Lit.—He having gone days how many gone ?

He has been absent two days.
Shi yisi nchōk enni wō.
Lit.—He having gone day's two gone.

You are taller than I.
Aiyo ni sapō wō.
Lit.—I you tall gone or become.

2.—COMPARISON OF ADJECTIVES.

(1) *Comparative.*—When two objects are compared in a declarative sentence, the adjective takes the participial affix *wō* = "gone,"

"become", sometimes for euphony *mō* or *o*, and the subject of the expression is placed after the object with which the comparison is made: *e.g.*—

You are taller than I.
Aiyō ni sapō wō.

Lit.—I you tall gone or become.

You eat more than I.
Aiyō nī khyangwō tsōālā.

Lit.—I you hard gone eat.

I am taller than you.
Nnā ā rāmō.

Lit.—You I old become.

This is better than that.
Shīcho chī mhōmō.

Lit.—This that good gone or become.

In interrogative sentences comparisons are denoted by repeating the adjective, first, with the participial affix *wō*, *mō*, or *o* followed by the interrogative affix *ālo*; and, secondly, with the same participial affix followed by the interrogative affix *ēlā* :—

Which is the better, Kohima or Wokha?
Kōhime mhōmōālo Wōkhe mhōmōēlā?

Which are the better, cows or horses?
Māngsü mhōmōālo korr mhōmōēlā?

Cows are better.
Māngsü mhōmō.

Are you the taller, or am I the taller?
Nī sapōālo, ā sapōēlā?

I am the taller; you are the shorter.
Ā sapōwō; nī hendrōwō.

Is this the sweeter or is that the sweeter?
Shī enangōālo chī enangoēlā?

This is sweeter.
Shī enangwō.

(2) *Superlative.*—The superlative degree is expressed by using the pronominal adjective "all", or a numeral indicating the whole number of objects under consideration before the name of the

individual supposed to possess the quality *par excellence*, together with the adjective with the affix *wō, mō, o*:—

This is the largest boy.

Langā nūngōr shi tsapōwō.

Lit.—All boys this large gone or become.

This is good, this is good, but this is the best of all.

Shī mhō, shī mhō, tōāhā lāngā shī mhōmō.

Lit.—This good, this good, but all this good gone or become.

3.—NUMERALS.

(1) CARDINALS.

1—*Ekhā.*
2—*Enni.*
3—*Etham.*
4—*Mezü.*
5—*Mūngo.*
6—*Tīrōk.*
7—*Ti-ing, tscang.*
8—*Tizā.*
9—*Tōkū.*
10—*Taro, tarå, tero.*
11—*Taro sü*, or *si ekhā.*
12—*Taro sü enni.*
13—*Taro sü etham.*
14—*Taro sü mezü.*
15—*Taro sü mūngo.*
16—*Taro sü tirōk.*
17—*Taro sü tiing.*
18—*Taro sü tizā.*
19—*Taro sü tōkū*
20—*Mekwī*, or *mekwü.*
21—*Mekwü sü ekha.*
22—*Mekwü sü etham*, &c., &c.
30—*Thamdro.*
40—*Züro.*
50—*Tiingyā.*
60—*Rōkro.*
70—*Ekhā tscang, ekhā tiing.*
80—*Ekhā tizā.*
90—*Ekhā tōkū.*
100—*Ekhā tāro*=*nzo, nzü.*
1,000—*Thāngā.*

Notes on the Numerals.

Among the Lhōtās counting is done on the fingers and toes, and as far as possible, by tens.

Tally is kept by the use of small sticks or on strings of large beans.

Ekhā = one, is used only in counting. When single objects are specified, *nchyūā, matsangā* and *ntsangā* = "one," are used instead of *ekhā; nchyūā*, being applied only to human beings: *e. g.*—

One man = { *Kyōn̠ nchyūā.* / *Kyōn̠ matsangā.* / *Kyōn̠ ntsangā.* }

One cow = { *Māngsü matsangā.* / *Māngsü ntsangā.* }

Nine = *Tōkū* or *ekhānā tāto mpām.*

Lit.—By one ten wanting.

The particle *sü* like the word *krö* in Angāmī Nāgā means "added to," "increased," "more": *e.g.*—

Eleven = *Tāro sü ekhā.*

Lit.—Ten more one.

Give me one more = *Matsangā ā pisā.*

NOTE.—The vowel *ü* is here changed to *ā*, the regular ending of the imperative.

Sixteen = *Tāro sü tirōk* = Ten and six, or

Mezünā mekwü m-pen = By four twenty incomplete.

This latter method of counting is in general use among the Aō and Angāmī tribes. When the point between ten and twenty is reached, the mind seems to run forward to the succeeding ten and completes the calculation by mentioning the number of digits there are short of the higher number. The Lōhtās generally prefer the former method, although they frequently employ the latter. On reaching twenty-one they often call attention to the fact that thirty is the next ten, by saying *mekwü sü thamdrowe ckhā* = twenty and, toward thirty, one, after which they count on to thirty calling the digits in regular order, thus, *mekü sü enni* = twenty and two, &c. Then again in the same way.

They also sometimes proceed throughout by mentioning each time how many have been counted in the direction of the next ten, or how many their calculation falls short of it.

Thirty = *Thamdro* = "three tens," from *etham* = three and *tāro* = ten.

Forty = *Züro* = "four tens," from *mezü* = four and *tāro* = ten.

FRACTIONS.

One-half = *Pōko.*

One and one-half = *Matsangā sü pōko.*

One-third = *Echü etham chüche matsangā.*

Lit.—Parts three division one.

(2) ORDINALS.

(*A*) *Ordinal Adjectives.*

First = *Ovūngōchü* (the one in front).

Second = „ *sīlāmo* (the one in front behind).

Third = *Ovūngōchü chito ōnī silāmo* (the one in front that one two behind), &c., &c., or

Ennōāchü silāmo (the again behind).

(*B*) *Ordinal Adverbs.*

Once = *Chōā, echōā, echūngā.*
Twice = *Echōni, echūng ennī.*
Thrice = *Echōetham, echūng etham.*

(*C*) *Multiplicatives.*

Singly = *Mutsangtsangnā* (one by one).
By twos = *Ennī ninā* (two by two).
By threes = *Etham thamnā* (three by three).

PRONOUNS.

In Lhōtā Nāgā the case relations of pronouns are indicated by postpositions. The nominative and ablative cases take the affix *nā* under the same circumstances as do nouns. The sāme words are used for both masculine and feminine genders.

(1) Personal Pronouns.

Singular—
- I = *Ā, ai, aiyo, ākhā.*
- You = *Nā, nnā, nō, nnō, ninā, yi.*
- He, she, it = *Hi, shī, chi, chü.*

Plural—
- We = *E, ete.*
- You = *Ni, nino, nten, yi.*
- They = *Hiāng, shiāng, shiāno, chiāng chīāno, chüāng, ōtēn, ōnte.*

Shī enni = "we" in the expression "he and I."

Shī nā ā tō = he and I.

Eni = we (you and I).

Ni nā ā tō = you and I.

Ninī = You two.

Ōchi tō ōni = they two (at some distance).

Shi tō ōnī = these two (near at hand).

Personal Pronouns Illustrated.

I am calling = *Ānā tsālā.*

I don't go for wood = *Aiyo ōtsango m-mō.*

It is I = *Ākhā, Ākhānyū, Ālālā.*

The expression *Ā khānyū* seems to be about equal to the English expression "I, if you please."

I am hungry = *Ā wōntōntsangālā.*

I am tired = *Ā mōkthātā.*

I am sleepy = *Ai ying hngtātā.*

This is my property = *Shīcho ā tsakī.*

For genitive forms see under Possessive Pronouns:—

My brother is waiting for me in the road = *Ā tācho ā tsconā ōlāmenā ā hnyākāvānā.*

Come to me = *Ā thingi rōā.*

Did you buy this for me? = *Nno shīcho a tchü shıchonüng?*

Did he give it to you? = *Shīna chī ni pīpilā ?*

They are keeping this for you = *Ōtēnā nī etscōnā shī vātālā.*

It will be noticed that the dative of "you" always ends in *i*:—

We will beat them = *Enā shian tapvū.*

Will you go with them or not? = *Ntenā shiang pānā wōwōlā ?*

Let those two go = *Hetō ōni wōtōkā.*

When I was ill they came = *Ā pirapāthang hiano rōcho.*

They went some time ago = *Ōtenā ōsī wōcho.*

(2) Possessive Pronouns.

Possessive pronouns immediately precede the name of the object possessed: *e.g.*—

My house = *Ā ki.*

Your house = *Nī ki.*

His house = *Shī ki, ōmō kī.*

Our house = *Ekī, enki, etenki.*

Your house = *Nīn ki, nten ki.*

Their house = *Ōten kī, ōnte kī, chuāng ki, shiāng ki.*

The adjective "own," frequently found connected with the possessive case of the personal pronoun, is *ōmō, ōmōchi* :—

My own house = *Ā mōchi kī.*

Your own house = *Nī mōchi ki.*

His own house = *Ō mōchi kī.*

Our own house = *E mōchi ki.*

Your own house = *Nī mōmō ki.*

In case of a plurality of objects possessed, the word for "own" becomes *mōmōchi* or *mōmō* :—

Your own houses = *Nī mōmōchi ki.*
Their own houses = *Ō mōmōchi kī.*

(3) Demonstrative Pronouns.

The demonstrative pronouns are—

Singular— { *Shi, hi* = this.
Chī = that.

Plural— { *Shiāng shiāṉ* = these.
Ōteṉ ōteno, chiāng, chyūāṉ = those.

They are used both adjectively and substantively without change of form, and, as before remarked, *shi* and *chī* are employed for the definite article, and also for the third personal pronoun, singular, the latter being used as a relative in the formation of participial nouns and adjectives, and *shiang* and *chiang* are used for the third personal pronoun plural.

The words *nchyūā* = one, referring to individuals of the human species, and *matsangā* and *ntsangā* = one of any class of objects, often used to represent our indefinite pronoun, or the indefinite expression "a certain," may also be classed among demonstrative pronouns. These words may also be used adjectively or substantively without change of form :—

Yesterday a certain individual came = { *Nchö nchyūā rōcho.*
Nchö kyōṉ nchyūā rōcho.

(4) Interrogative Pronouns.

Who = *Ōchi, ōchō.*

Which = *Ōchō, kūwe, kō.*

What = *Ōchō, ōchi* (referring to persons),
ntīō, nyū, nyūwo (referring to things).

Who came? = *Ōchō rōchōlā?*

With whom did he come? = *Shi ōchi pānā rōchōlā?*

Whom did you call? = *Nnā ōchō tsāchōlā?*

Which boy did you beat? = *Nnō nūngōr ōcho* ("or" *kūwe*) *tāpchōlā*

Which "*dao*" will you take? = *Lepōk kūwe khiūla?*

Which of the three will you take? = *Nnō ōnthamo kō khiūlā?*

What is your name = { *Nī myang ōchī wēlā?* / *Nī myang ōchōlā?* }

What do you want? = *Nnō ntiō chōnālā?*

What is the matter? = { *Nyūwo tscōchōlā?* / *Ntiō chōlā?* / *Nyū chōlā?* }

What is this? = *Hicho nyūōlā?*

What are you searching for? = *Nnō ntiō yānālā?*

In whose house did he sleep? = *Hicho ōchōki yipchōlā?*

Whose necklace is this? = *Shicho ōcho yōkōlā?*

I don't know which is good nor which is bad = *Mhōm kū m-mhōm kūsānā ānā n-tsü.*

Relative Pronouns.

The relative pronoun in Lhōtā Nāgā is expressed either by the particle *chü*, *chi*="the one" affixed to verbal nouns and adjectives, or by the use of the interrogatives *ōchī*, *ōchō*="who" and *ku kuwe*="which," followed by the demonstrative this=*shī*, *hi*, or that=*hi chī*: *e.g.*—

The man who came yesterday.
Nchö kyōn erōwōchü.

Lit.—Yesterday man coming the one.

The child who died.
Nūngōr etchhüwōchī.

This is the horse which I sold.
Ānā korr eyemmōchü shī.

This is the cow that I said I would sell.
Ānā māngsü eyem ephyōwōchü shī.

Bring the book which is lying on the table.
Kāko pilang ōpōnī evanwōchü hānsī iyā.

Take the one which you like.
Kūwe nī khī hugānā chī khiā.

Lit.—Which you to take desiring that take.

The one who is coming is my brother, perhaps.
Ōcho rōānā chī ātā khāche.

Lit.—Who coming he my brother perhaps.

This is what I wanted.
Ānā echōmōchü shī.

Lit.—I wanting the one this.

Give me the one I wanted.
Ānā kūwe chōnānā chī āpiā.

Lit.—I what wanting that me give.

Compound or Indefinite Relatives.

Compound relatives are formed by reduplicating the single relatives and employing the particle *sānā*, a sign of indefiniteness. This particle appears as an affix to the verb or participle :—

Whoever wishes to go can go.

Ōchīchīnā wō hngāsānā chī wōtōkū.

Ōchīānnā wō hngāsānā chī wōtōkū.

Go by whichever road you wish.

Ōlāṉ kūe kūwe nī wōhngsānā chī wōā.

Whatever is bad don't eat.

Kū kū m-mho nānā chī tī tsōā.
Kūwe kūwe m-mho sānā chī tī tsōā.

Lit.—What what bad that not eat.

I will take whatever you give.
Nnā ntīō ntīō ā piāsānā ānā khiū.

Whether he will go or or not I do not know.
Hīnā wōsānā n-wosānā ānā n-tsü.

(6) Reciprocal Pronouns.

The reciprocal pronouns are formed by reduplicating the personal pronouns, or employing with a single personal pronoun the phrase "one by one" twice repeated :—

We strike each other.
Enī enī tāptātā.
Enī nchyūānā nchyūā tāv, nchyūānā nchyūā tāv.

We love one another.
Ete ete lamtālā.

Why do you steal from each other ?
Nini ntsōle nchyuānā nchyūā tsāk efū nchyūānā nchyūā tsāke efū.

They killed one another.
Ōten ōten nangtācho.

NOTE.—The verbal particle *tā* affixed to verbal roots indicates that several individuals are engaged in an act.

(7) REFLEXIVE PRONOUNS.

The compound personal or reflexive pronouns are formed by affixing *mōchi* or *mōmō* = "self" to the simple forms of the personal pronoun :—

I broke it myself = *Āmōchinā shi khirapcho.*

You saw it yourself = *Nimochinā shi hüngcho.*

He ate it himself = { *Shimōchinā chi tsōchō.* / *Ōmōchinā chi tsōcho.* }

I struck myself = *A mōmō tāpcho.*

They killed themselves = { *Ōmōmōnā nangthācho.* / *Shian mōmōnā nangthācho.* }

Did you hurt yourself ? = *Nimōmo ōtsako enōmpāpchoke ?*

You yourselves killed the fowl = *Nite mōmōnā hōno sātācho.*

(8) INDEFINITE PRONOUNS AND PRONOMINAL ADJECTIVES.

A, certain = *Nchyūā, ōyān, matsangā, ntsanga.*

All = *Ōmpā, hālāngto, lāngā, hetōpū, hetōpāū.*

Anybody = *Ōyān, ōchīhā.*

Anything = *Ntiō, nyūsānā, nyūwōsānā, lāmālamā, lamāthangterro.*

How many / How much } = *Kōtā, kūtā.*

No one = *Ōchīhā* (with negative form of the verb).

Nothing = *Ntīhā, nyūhā* (with negative form of the verb).

Many / Much } = *Elam, kōshā.*

Of this kind = *Hetuv.*

Of that kind = *Chituv.*

One = *Nchyūā, matsangā, ntsangā.*

Other, another = *Ōyān, thāmpho.*

Somebody }
Some one } = *Ōyan, ōchōsā.*

Something = *Ntiōsānā, nyūsānā, nyūwōsānā.*

So much }
So many } = *Hetātā, hetā, chitā.*

Such = *Hetuv, chituv.*

This much }
That much } = *Hetātā, chitātā.*

Illustrative Sentences.

A certain one said that you were a liar.	= { *Ōyānā phyōcho nno tācho ephyōe làto.* *Ōyānā phyōcho nno echang ephyōe làto.*
Yesterday a certain individual came to your house.	= *Nchö ni ki nchyūā rōcho.*
They are all here . . .	= { *Lāngā* / *Ōmpā* / *Hālāngtō* } *hello vāndrāvā.*
Give me another . . .	= *Thāmpho ā piā.*
I did not break it, another person broke it.	= *Ānā shi n-khirap ōyānā khirapcho.*
Is there anybody there or not?	= *Ōchi ōyāṉ vāvānilā?*
Has anybody come or not?	= *Ōchihā yiyilā?*
Have you anything to sell or not?	= { *Ntihā* / *Ntiōsānā* / *Nyūsānā* / *Lāmā lāmā* / *Lamāthangterro* } *eyem lililā?*
Let them both go . . .	= *Heto ōni wōtōkā.*
How many houses are there in your village?	= *Ni yāncho ōki kōtālā?*
What (how much) is the price of this?	= *Shicho kūtā māṉlā?*
There is no one here . . .	= *Hello ōchihā m-mā.*

He gave me nothing . .	= *Hinā nyūhā ā n-pi.*
There are many bamboos near our village.	= *Eyāni yānchōe puhrü elam liā.*
There is much "dhan" this year.	= { *Nchikamcho ōtsōk kōshā liā.* *Nchikamcho ōtsōk elam liā.*
Bring me this kind of "dhan"	= *Ōtscang hetüv hānsī rōā.*
I will not buy that kind .	= *Ghiluv ānā n-shiū.*
Give me one . . .	= *Matsangā ā piā.*
There is only one individual here and only one there.	= *Hello nchyūā ōchi nchyūā tō, te.*
Others who say they will sell fowls can sell them, I will not sell.	= *Oyānā hōno eyem ephyōwōtuvhāḳā chitüvnā yemkā, aiyo n-yen.*
Others can eat dogs, I will not eat them.	= *Ōyānā phuro tsōkā, aiyo n-tso.*
These oranges are good, but the others there are bad.	= *Kōngkeṉ hīcho mhōnā tōsu thāmpo chīcho m-mho.*
Some one is there . .	= *Ōchī ōchiosānā vānā.*
Give me something for this sore.	= *Emhōā shi etscōnā nyuwōsānā ā piā.*
I have a few cattle . .	= *A mangsü terrāro liā.*
Give me some (a little) . .	= *Etchakāro ā piā.*
I can not give so much (price)	= *Ōmāṉ hetācho ānā n-pikōk.*
There were so many others here we did not converse.	= *Ōyān hetā vāncho ennī n-chāntā.*
I have no mind to deal with such a man.	= *Kyōn hetuv thencho nyūhā ā n-shitā hng.*
Bring this kind of cloth .	= *Ōscü hetuv hānsi īyā.* *Ōscü shi essā hānsī īyā.*

NOTE.—*Essá* = like, resembling.

THE VERB.

In Lhōtā Nāgā the verb undergoes no change for the person and number of its subject. Moods, voices and tenses are indicated either by verbal affixes or by the context, and, as in Ao Nāgā, the verb freely enters into composition with other root words, which in a variety of ways modify its meaning. As will be seen, the Lhōtā verb fairly expresses the relations of time.

We will trace the verb *tsō* = "to eat" through the various moods and tenses. As will be observed, much freedom is allowed in the use of tenses, and, as in other languages of this type, the forms employed are far from being used with absolute consistency.

INDICATIVE MOOD.

Present Tense.
Present Imperfect.
Past Imperfect.

Often no distinction is made in the formation of these three tenses, the context being regarded a sufficient guide as to the time of the action.

The form thus common to these three tenses is the verbal root with the affix *ā* followed by the still further affix *lā*. This latter affix is one form of the verb *liā* = "is":—

Present Tense— . I always eat rice.
Nchōkāpaṉ ānā ōtsī tsōālā.

Lit.—Always I rice eating am.

Present Imperfect— . I am eating now.
Nthāngā ānā tsōālā.

Lit.—Now I eating am.

Past Imperfect— . When the Sahab came yesterday I was eating.
Nchō etsi rōāthang chithangchō ānā tsōālā.

Lit.—Yesterday Sahab coming time, that time I was eating.

The present tense is also indicated by the simple root. This is also the form for the future. This form of the verb is most commonly used when several customary or universal acts are mentioned in succession: *e.g.*—

I eat rice, vegetables and meat.
Ānā ōtsī tsō, ōhāṉ tsō, ōsō tsō.

Lit.—I rice eat, vegetables eat, meat eat.

In enumerations like this both the above-mentioned forms of the verb are employed, thus—

Ao Nāgās eat dogs, Angāmī Nāgās eat dogs, Lhōtā Nāgās eat dogs, all Nāgās eat dogs.

Chamhā phūrro tsō, Tsangōhą phūrro tsō, Kyōṉha phūrro tsō, lāngānā phūrro tsōālā.

When the continuity of an act is especially in mind, the verbal root with *ā* is followed by the verb *vān* = "is," in the sense of continuing, in its various tenses: thus—

I am eating = *Ānā tsōā vānālā.*

Lit.—I to eat am continuing.

Yesterday I was eating = *Nchö ānā tsōā vānā.*

Lit.—Yesterday I to eat was continuing.

When the Sahab came yesterday I was eating = *Nchö etsi roathangcho ānā tsōā vāncho.*

Lit.—Yesterday Saheb coming time I to eat was continuing or continued eating.

NOTE.—The verb *vān* signifies "stay" "remain," "continue," "live," "abide," "is" in the sense of continuing, "have": thus—

Is the Sahab in or not? = *Etsi vāvānilā?*

He is not in = *M-mā*, or *n-vān.*

Have you a wife? = *Ni elué vāvānila?*

I live there = *Ānā ōchi vānā.*

The present imperfect is also indicated by the verbal root with *ā*, and the still further affix *kamā* = "is" "being." This affix seems to be still another form of the verb *liā* = "is": *e.g.*—

I am eating rice = *Ānā ōtsi tsōā kamā.*

Lit.—I rice eating am.

NOTE.—The affix *kamā* more frequently occurs in participial forms.

Past Tense.—The past tense of the verb is indicated either by the verbal root with the affix *ā* or by the verbal root with the affix *cho*—

I ate = { *Ānā tsōā.* / *Ānā tsōcho.* }

Present Perfect Tense.—The present perfect tense is indicated either by the verbal root with the affix *ā* or the verbal root with the affix *chākā*, *e.g.*—

He has eaten = { *Shinā tsōā.* / *Shinā tsōchākā.* }

Past Perfect Tense.—The past perfect tense is the same in form with the present perfect tense, the context being relied upon to indicate the completion of the act in past time:—

When the Sahab came I had eaten = { *Etsi rōāthangcho ānā tsōchākā.* }

This tense is also indicated by a reduplication of the affix *chākā*, in which case the completion of the act is considered as having taken place in time less remote than that indicated by the simple affix : *e.g.*—

I had eaten = { *Ānā tsōchākchākā.* / *Ānā tsōchākā.* }

More time, however, has elapsed since the latter act.

Future Tense.—The future tense is indicated either by the simple verbal root or the verbal root with the affix *kā*. The former is the more common :—

I will eat = { *Ānā tsō.* / *Ānā tsōkā.* }

A mute *v* or the vowel *u* is sometimes heard at the close of future affirmatives :—

I will eat = *Ānā tsōv.*
I will call = *Ānā tsau.*

Still further the verbal root with the affix *sālā* refers to a near future, and in some connections is hardly distinguishable from the present : thus—

Ānā tsōsālā = I am on the point of eating.

Before passing to the other moods we will illustrate negative and interrogative forms.

NEGATIVE FORMS.

Negative forms are indicated by prefixing *n* or *m* to the verb, except in the imperative mood, where the particle *ti* is used.

These negative prefixes must generally be pronounced as separate syllables, and always on a higher key than the rest of the word :—

I do not eat. =
I am not eating =
I was not eating =
} *Ānā n-tsō.* / *Ānā tsōā m-mān̲.*

Here *m-mān̲* is only another form for *n-vān*, the letters, *n* and *v* being changed to "*m*" for the sake of euphony—

I was not eating = { *Ānā n-tsōākā.* / *Ānā n-tsōāvānā.* / *Ānā n-tsōā vāncho.* }

I have not eaten =
I had not eaten =
} *Ānā n-tsōāhā.*

I will not eat = *Ānā n-tsō.*
Do not eat = *Ti tsōā.*

Interrogative Forms.

Single interrogatives that can be answered by "yes" or "no," are indicated by the particles *ke* or *nung,* while an indirect question is indicated by the particle *lā.* These particles occur as affixes, *ke* occurring more commonly with the present, past and future tenses, and *nung* with the past imperfect, present perfect and past perfect tenses. Double interrogatives reduplicate the verbal root and affix *ālā*, or the verbal root is repeated, first with *ālō*, and secondly in a negative form with the affix *ālā.*

In Lhōtā Nāgā the voice always falls at the close of a question; and in double interrogatives, where the verb is reduplicated, the first syllable of the reduplication is spoken on a much higher key than the rest of the word:—

Do you eat? = { *Nnō tsōāke?* / *Nnō tsōānung?* }

Do you eat or not? = *Nnō tsō tsōālā?*

Do you eat or do you not eat? = *Nnō tsōālo n-tsōālā?*

Are you eating? = { *Nnā tsōālā nung?* or *Nnā tsōā vānā nung?* }

Did you eat? = *Nnō tsōchōke?*

Did you eat or not? = *Nnō tsō tsōēlā?*

Did you eat or did you not eat? = *Nnō tsō tsōālo, n-tsōchōlā?*

It will be seen that in the past tense the connecting vowel of the double interrogative is *ē* instead of *ā* as in the present tense:—

Have you eaten = } *Nnā tsōchākānung?*
Had you eaten = }

Had you eaten? = *Nnā tsōchākchākānung?*

Have you eaten or not? = *Nnā tsōtsōhālā?*

Will you eat? = *Nnō tsōke?*

Will you eat or not = *Nnō tsōtsōālā?*

When permission is asked *ne* is the sign of interrogation, *e.g.*, Can I go? = *Ānā yiāne?* This form of interrogation is equivalent to the English expression "Did you say that I could go" or "Am I permitted to go?"

IMPERATIVE MOOD.

Like the present tense of the indicative mood, the present and future imperative are formed by affixing *ā* to the verbal root—

Eat = *Tsōā.*

Tī is the sign of negation in this mood—

Do not eat = *Tī tsōā.*

SUBJUNCTIVE MOOD.

In Lhōtā Nāgā condition and concession are generally expressed by means of participial phrases followed, in the clause expressing the conclusion, by a verb in its regular form—

If you eat this you will be well = *Nnā shī tsōnā pō.*

Although you eat I will not eat = *Nnā tsōlehā, ānā n-tsō.*

Go and see whether the cow eats her "dhan" or not = { *Māngsü ōtsōk tsō tsōāsānā wō zetā.* / *Māngsü ōtsōk tsōālo n-tsōā sānā wō zetā.* }

For further illustrations, see under Participles and Conjunctions.

The potential subjunctive is formed by adding *wō* to the verbal root of the protasis and *kātōlā* to the verbal root of the apodosis—

If rice were here, I would eat = *Ōtsi hello vānwō, ānā tsō kàtōlā.*

If you had eaten it, you would have known whether it was good or bad = *Nnā shī tsōwō, mhōm m-mhōm ntsyūkàtōlā.*

If I had wished I could have eaten = *Ānā tsōhngwo, tsō-chākūkàtōlā.*

If you had come yesterday I would have eaten. = *Nnā nchō rōwō ānā tsōkàtōlā.*

The particles of ambiguity *escā* and *sānyu* signifying "perhaps" are used with the different forms of the verb to indicate the uncertainty of an act—

I may eat = *Ānā tsō escā.*

Lit.—I will eat perhaps.

It may rain = { *Erū chō escā.* / *Erū chōescūkā.* / *Erū chōsānyū.* }

Lit.—It will rain perhaps.

POTENTIAL MOOD.

Potentials are formed by adding the particles *kōk* and *che* to the verbal root. The particle *che* frequently denotes that the power to perform an act is dependent upon the will of another :—

NOTE.—The final *k* of the particle *kōk* is a mute consonant.

Can you eat or can you not eat? = *Nnā tsō kōkūālo n-tsō kōkūālā?*

I cannot eat = { *Ānā n-tsōkōk.* / *Ānā n-tsōche.* }

I can eat it = { *Ānā tsōkōkā.* / *Ānā tsōcheyū.* }

I cannot walk without a cane. { = *Chārōng m-pānā ōlān n-tsāche.* / = *Chāgōng m-pānā ōlān n-tsākōk.* }

Can I eat this rice? = *Ānā ōtsi hi tsōkūkānūng?*

You can eat it = *Nnā hi tsōkōkā.*

NOTE.—In asking permission *ne* is generally the interrogative particle employed—

May I eat? = *Ānā tsōāne.*

This seems to be a polite way of asking permission, and is something like the English expression "Please may I eat?" or "Did you say that I might eat?" The answer in the same vein would be *Tsōnā-te khānyū* = "Eat if you like."

Compulsion or permission is denoted also by the causal affix *tōk*—

You can eat afterwards, *Ōkhānāti ni tsōtōkū.* } *i.e.*, you will be allowed to eat afterwards.

See Causative Forms.

VOICE.

As in Āō and Angāmi Nāgā, the Lhōtā verb has no distinct passive form. The forms of the perfect and past perfect tenses of the indicative mood may be used in either an active or passive sense, according to the construction of the sentence—

Active voice—{ I have eaten my rice. / *Ātsi ānā tsōchākā.* }

Passive voice—{
The rice which was (in that) there yesterday has been eaten.
Nchō ōtsi chilo evāṉwōchi tsōchākā.
This is broken = *Chi khirapchakā.*
It was broken before I gave it to you.
Ānā ni piwōchi vūngina khirapchaka.
The dog was killed yesterday.
Nchō phuro sātāchākā. }

The particle *chākā* is also used with intransitive verbs—

He has come = *Hinā yichākā.*

The tree has fallen = *Ōtông yiāchākā.*

Predicate Adjectives.

With predicate adjectives signifying bodily or mental states, the copula appears in the affixes *ā, tā, tātā, tsangā.*

I am ill . = *Ā phiraptātā.*
I was ill . = *Ā phirāpā.*
I have been ill = *Ā phiraptsangā.*

I was ill = *Ā phiraptācho.*

I have been ill. = *Ā phirapte vāncho.*

I am hungry . = *Ā wōntōnā.*
I was hungry . = *Ā wōntōntātā.*
I have been hungry *Ā wōntōntsangā.*

Are you sleepy? = { *Nī ying hngtsangchōke?* / *Nī ying hngtāchoke?* / *Nī ying hngtātā nüng?* }

Yes, I am sleepy = { *Ho, aiyo ying hngtātā.* / *Ho, aiyo ying tsangā.* }

Infinitive.

The naked root in the simple verb in Lhōtā does not correspond to the infinitive in English, nor is it to be confounded with the participle, since it partakes of the nature neither of a noun nor an adjective. It may be translated either by the present participle or the simple verb followed by the conjunction "and," the same as in Assamese.

The latter form gives the most exact sense: *e.g.*—

I eating slept . / I ate and slept . } = *Ānā tsō yipcho.*

I am eating and drinking = *Ānā tsō yūālā.*

Eating drink . / Eat and drink . } = *Tsō yūā.*

Going eat . / Go and eat . } = *Ōyi tsōā.*

Coming eat . / Come and eat . } = *Ōrō tsōā.*

Note.—Here the words for 'go' and 'come' each assume the prefix *ō*, which is a very common prefix with a large class of nouns; as *ōki* = house, *ōmā* = salt, *ōtsi* = rice, &c., &c. (See Note 3 under Classification of Nouns.)

GERUNDS.

The following forms may perhaps be best classified as gerunds—

(1) The verbal root with the affix *kàttō* or *kiàttō* :

I wish to eat = *Ānā tsō kiàttō tscōālā.*

He came to eat with me = *Hīnā ā thenī tsō kiàtto yicho.*

(2) The verbal root with the affix *lō*, or with both the affix *lō* and the prefix *e*, or with simply the prefix *e*—

I came to eat = { *Ānā tsōlō rōcho.* / *Ānā etsōlō rōcho.* / *Ānā etsō rōcho.* }

I wish to go to eat, *i.e.*, for the purpose of eating—

Ānā tsōlō wōkiàtto tscōālā.

The above forms seem for the most part to be used interchangeably. In expressions of purpose, however, I am inclined to think the latter forms are the more common.

Purpose may also be expressed by the use of the participle *kamā* = "being," followed by a conjunction or even without the conjunction :—

I am going very early in order to reach Wokha to day.

Nching Wōkhā chām kamā hi etscōnā ānā nyāzanginā wō.

Lit.—To-day Wokha being reached for this I very early will go.

The above sentence with the gerund forms would read—

Nching Wokhā echām or *chāmkiàttō nyāzanginā wō.*

PARTICIPLE.

As in other languages of this type, participial expressions are a favourite style of structure. Connectives are little used, and long sentences consist almost wholly of adverbial and postpositional phrases and participial expressions, as will be seen from the following illustrations :—

Efwinā Wōkhā etsi māngsü efwi sōsi yiā vānle Wokhā etsīnā korr mānkwinā Kōhime thrōwā vānle, ōlāmīnā mhūngi tsangīnā thiāpānāhā n-thihrāk ōre sānte sicho. Kyōnā ōchōte Kangchi yilo ewenā mhūngikhi rhamī hānsiro sepe pile sepenā tapsü ōchōe yōnchāk theyisi vangālā.

Lit.—A thief Wokha Sahab's cow stealing, having bound, while going along, Wokha Sahab pony's back upon, to Kohima while going over, from the path seeing, with a gun even shooting, did not hit. To the jungle fled. A Naga the next day, Kangchī (name of village) to the cultivation of on going, getting a sight of, catching, bringing to the sepoys gave. The sepoys having beaten, on his legs fetters having put, are keeping in confinement.

Kyōnā rōnā ni māngsü kūlātō āngānā emyamōchi Kūlai sōsi chōwō yenchākā, emhū wōchi hello vānā tō ezōkā.

Lit.—A Naga coming your cows where me asking, the red one to Golaghat being led down has been sold, the white one here is, saying, will tell.

Aiyō hellōnā Kōhīme thrōwosi, chichōro ntsāngā vānsi Kūlai chōwōsi chūngchenā Bundār lāninā chūngyiū.

Lit.—I from here to Kohimā having gone over, there month one after staying, to Golaghat having gone down, from there by the Bundar road will come up.

Having taken this and placed it there, taking a rupee and going quickly down to the bazaar buy your brother a good cloth and bring it up to the house here.

Shī hānsi ōchi vānsi ōrāng matsangā hānsi bōzare ekhiō lākā chōwō nitā etchü oscü mhōm shi hānsi ōkī hello chūng yiā.

It will be seen from the above that the Nagas very often omit the subject of succeeding clauses after they have once been mentioned, and depend largely upon the context to suggest the tense of participial expressions.

The following short sentences will illustrate the more general uses of Lhōtā participles :—

(1) Verbal root with the affix *nā :*

If you eat this you will be ill = *Shī tsōnā ni pirapthau.*

Eating this causes me pain = *Shī tsōnā ā saptōkālā.*

Nā is also added to adjective roots, thus—

This being bad how can I eat ? = *Shicho m-mhōnā kōtōli tsōvlā ?*

(2) Verbal root with affix *i :*

He seeing me struck me = *Hinā ā mhūngi ā tāpcho.*

(3) Verbal root with affix *ā* and postposition *thang*=" at the time of," "while."

While I eating I saw a tiger=*Anā tsōāthang mhorr mhūngā.*

This same postposition is used with a negative verbal form to denote the precedence of an action—

I cannot go before eating = *Anā n-tsoāthang cho n-wōkōk.*

(4) Verbal root with *ā* and affix *le* or *vanle*—

While I was eating I saw a tiger=*Anā tsoa vānle mhorr mhūngā.*

While going along in the path I saw a tiger=*Anā ōlāni wōle mhorr mhūngā.*

(5) Verbal root with affix *sānāti*, sign of futurity—

On having eaten your rice go to the bazaar = *Ni tsi tsōā-sānāti wōā.*

(6) Verbal root with affix *si* or *sā*—

The tiger having caught and eaten the man has fled=*Mhorr-nā kyōn rhami tsōsā tsāncho.*

Having eaten / After eating } come=*Tsōsi rōā.*

(7) Verbal root with affix *chāknā* :

After having eaten my rice I will go=*Â tsi tsōchāknā wō.*

Having eaten this go = *Shi tsōchāknā iyā.*

This having been eaten what shall we do? = *Shi tsōchāknā eninā kūtā lyūlā.*

(8) Verbal root with affixes *lehā, chāklā,* denoting concession :

Although he eats this he cannot get well = *Shi tsōlehā m-pōkōku.*

Although I ate rice yesterday, I'll eat potatoes to-day=*Nchōānā ōtsī tsōchōlehā nchingo ānā hōrō tsō.*

Since you have eaten why are you hungry?=*Ōtsi tsōchāklā nyūtsōle ni wōntōnālā?*

VERBAL MODIFIERS.

It has already been remarked that the simple Lhōtā verb freely takes on syllables which modify its meaning in a variety of ways. These modifying syllables or root words, the origin of some of which are clearly traceable, while that of others has become quite obscure, appear both as prefixes and affixes to the verbal root. The following are examples :—

Affixes.

(1) Causative Verbs—

Causative verbs are indicated by the affix *tōk*—

I am causing him to eat = *Ànā hi tsōtōkālā.*

He caused me to go = *Shinā ā wōtōkcho.*

He has been caused to go = *Hi wōtōkchākā.*

Cause him to come = *Shi rōtōkā.*

(2) Permissives are identical in form with causatives—

Let him go = *Shi wōtōkā.*

Let him eat = *Shi tsōtōkā.*

NOTE.—It should be remembered that the sign of interrogation with permissives is generally *ne* : *e.g.*—

Did you say that I could eat ? = *Ānā tsōāne ?*

(3) Desideratives are indicated by the affix *hng* and *tāne*—

I wish to eat = *Ā tsōhngā.*

I do not wish to eat = *Ā n-tsōhng.*

Let us eat = *Eni tsōtāne.*

(4) Frequentatives are indicated by the adverbial prefix *n-sāṉ-nsām,* and by the verbal root reduplicated with the affix *pvū*—

He eats frequently = { *Shinā n-sāṉ nsām tsōālā.* / *Hinā tsōpvū tsōpvū vānālā.* }

(5) The continuity of an action is denoted by the verb *vān.* See under present and imperfect tenses—

He was eating = *Hinā tsōā vāncho.*

He is continuing to eat = *Hinā tsōā vānāla.*

(6) The affix *lān* or *lām* signifies repetition and return—

I will eat again = *Ānā tsōlām.*

Eat again = *Tsōlānā.*

He came again = *Hinā rōlāncho.*

Will you come back again ? = *Nnā elānai iyūlā ?*

I gave it back to him = *Ānā shi pilancho.*

(7) The affix *tem* or *ten* indicates the first doing of an act—

I ate first = *Ānā tsotencho.*

The boy who came first got the orange = *Nüngör rōtemōchī kōngken khīcho.*

(8) The affix *sālā* indicates the beginning of an act, or that it is about to be accomplished. This affix is added to the future form—

I am about to eat
I am beginning to eat } = *Ānā tsōvsālā.*

I am about to go = *Ānā wōsālā.*

The child is beginning to cry = *Ngāro kiāpvūsālā.*

(9) The verbal root repeated with the affix *phen* denotes regularity—

I eat regularly = *Ā tsōphen ā tsōphenī tsōālā.*

(10) The affixes *tā* and *rā* denote that several individuals are engaged in an act—

We love each other = *Eninā eyilōtālā.*

They are eating together = *Ōtenā tsōtālā.*

(11) The affix *khān* signifies all, and thus to complete—

I have eaten all = *Ānā tsōkhānchākā.*

I have done all the work = *Ānā nsundrū khānchākā.*

Eat it all = *Hī tsōkhānā.*

(12) The affix *nhyūa"* signifies incompleteness—

I have partly eaten the rice = *Ānā ōtsi tsōnhyūa.*

The same is indicated by means of the affix *khan* with a negative: *e.g.*—

I have not eaten all the rice = *Ānā ōtsi n-tsōkhān.*

(13) The affix *sā* indicates more—

Give me more = *Ā pisā.*

(14) The affix *hrāk* signifies to get—

I got some beef to eat = *Ānā māngsü sō tsōhrākā.*

I got a sight of him = *Ānā shi mhūnghrākā.*

(15) The affixes *kōk* and *che* denote ability—

He being ill cannot eat = *Hinā pirapthākamā n-tsōkōk.*

I can go now = *Nthangā ānā wōcheū.*

See Potential Mood.

(16) The affix *che* denotes probability—

I may eat = *Ānā tsōcheū.*

He may go = *Hinā wōcheū.*

See Subjunctive Mood.

(17) The affix *lō* signifies "along," "on" in the sense of continuing—

Come along = *Rōālō, rōālo.*

Go along = *Wōalō, wōālō.*

Eat on = *Tsōālō, tsōālō.*

(18) The affix *khāchi* with the verb *ze* = to see, directs the attention upwards, and in like manner the affix *chōchi* directs the attention downwards—

Look up = *Zekāchiā.*

Look down = *Zechōchiā.*

(19) The affix *hā* is often used to emphasize the action of the verb. An action may also be emphasized by doubling the verb—

He has surely not arrived there = *Shinā ōchi n-chahā.*

(20) The affixes *tsangā*, *khangā* and *tātā* are very frequently used with verbs, and denote either frequency or intensity of an act—

I am very sleepy = { *Ai yiptsangā.* / *Ai yiptātā.* }

He keeps beating me = *Hinā ā tāpkhangā.*

He is very cross = *Hi lamm tsōkhangā.*

I am very hungry = { *Ā wōntōntsangā.* / *Ā wōntōntātā.* }

(21) The particles *te* and *tai* signify "precisely," "exactly," "enough," "closely," "nearly," neither more nor less than is stated—

There is one here. That is all = *Hello matsangā. Te.*

Is there more there? There is no more = *Chīcho ennōāhā līlīlā? Tai.*

He gave me only two. That is all = *Hinā enni ti āpicho. Te.*

For the affix *ti* signifying "only," see under Nouns, Note 1, after Locative Case.

Prefixes.

(1) The prefix *chūng* signifies direction upward—

I will go up to Wokha = *Ānā Wōkhe chūngwō.*

Climb the tree=*Ōtōngwe chūngwōā.*

Mount the horse=*Korr māngkwi chūngwōā.*

(2) The prefix *chō* signifies direction downward—

Go down to the bazaar=*Shishopheni chōwōā.*

Dismount from the pony=*Korr māngkwenā chōyiā.*

He came down from the mountain=*Hicho phūnglāninā chōrōcho.*

(3) The prefixes *thrō* and *thre* signify direction "in". Direction from the plains is "in"; direction toward the plains is "out," the same as in English—

Come in = *Thre yiā.*

I am going into Kohima=*Ānā Kōhīme thre yiālā.*

I will go into Kohima=*Ānā Kōhīme thrōwō.*

NOTE.—The prefix *thre* is used with forms in *yiā* of the verb "to go" and *thrō* with forms in *wō* of the same verb.

(4) The prefix *chī* signifies out—

Go out = *Chiyiā.*

Let us go out to Wokha tomorrow?=*Enī ōchö Wòkhe chīyi tāne?*

(5) The prefixes *chū*, *shung*, *enhyī* signifying "against," are used with the common verbal form *kātā*, signifying contact: *e.g.*—

The pony ran against the fence=*Korrnā yūngāwō pāhrīlo chūkātā.*

I threw this against the door=*Ānā shi hānkānā shūngkātā.*

I accidentally struck my elbow against the chair—*Ānā m-mhūngwō ā khechüken khoktepheno chūkātā.*

Don't lean against me=*Ā ti enhyīkātā.*

VERBAL SYNONYMS.

The Lhōtā language like the Ao is rich in verbs, which denote variations of the same act: thus—

Ephyopālā=wash or cleanse in general.
Etsiālā = „ (clothes).
Süālā = „ (dishes).
Myūālā = „ (face).
Phīālā = „ (feet).
Ntsakālā = „ (hands).

Etymology of certain Verbs.

(1) The verb "go" has two roots, *yi* and *wō*.

To ascertain in certain expressions why one of these roots is used, and not the other, is often a difficult task. At times they seem to be used as exact synonyms. *Wō*, however, is nearly always used when the thought of a return, more or less remote, is in mind, except in the present perfect tense, where the root *yi* is employed: *e.g.*—

I will go to my house (the thought of returning not in mind).
Ānā ā ki yiū.

I will go to the Sahab's house (expecting to return).
Ānā etsi ki wō.

I will go to my village (not to return) = *Ē yāni wō.*

Where did he go? = *Shīcho kūi wōchōlā?*

He went to the Sahab's house = *Etsī kī wōcho.*

He has gone to the Sahab's house = *Etsī kī yichākā.*

He has gone for water = *Hicho ōtchhūlo yiā.*

(2) The verb "come" has three roots, *rō*, *yi*, and *tsā*—

(*a*) The root *rō* is the simplest form of the verb "to come."

He is coming = *Hi rōālā.*

I came yesterday = *Nchö ānā rōcho.*

He has come = *Hinā rōchākā.*

Don't come this way = *Hepōmwe ti rōā.*

Am I permitted to come in? = *Ānā tāchūngi thrọ rōāne?*

Don't let him come in now = *Nthāngā hī tī thrō rōtōkā*

(*b*) The root *yī* when signifying to come combines with it also the idea of a previous going, and may, perhaps, be termed preterito present, as it conveys the thought of the action as lying partly in the past and partly in the present: *e.g.*—

I (having been) am coming = *Ānā yiālā.*

I (having gone) will come = *Ānā yiū.*

When will you (having gone) come? = *Kōthang yiūlā.*.

The *yi* signifying "to come" is pronounced on a higher key than the same verb when it signifies to go. As in other words, there is sometimes a transposition of the letters of this root for the sake of euphony, and we have *īyā* instead of *yīā.*

(*c*) The verb *tsā* signifying "to come" is defective. It is used only of incomplete action. The same root signifies "to call." The verb *tsā* = "to come" is doubtless intimately connected in thought with the idea of calling—

He is coming (on the way) = { *Hī tsātā.* / *Hī tsātālā.* }

I have come (but not yet fully arrived at the point of destination) = *Ānā tsāchākā.*

(3) The auxiliary verbs "be," "have."—These verbs appear under several forms:

(*a*) The verb *lī* is the simplest form of the verb "to be." When standing alone it generally appears with the affix *ā*, and when used as an auxiliary, the *ī* is dropped, and the verb appears as the affix *lā* or *ālā*, *cho* and *chākā.*

In the early stages of the language the *ī* of the root was doubtless retained, but for the sake of euphony, or on account of carelessness in pronunciation, was soon dropped: *e.g.*—

I have two ponies, you have three ponies, together we have five = *Ā korr ennī lī nī korr etham lī tō ennī tsōtsī mūngoālā.*

It is there = *Ōchī līā.*

It was there = *Ōchī līcho.*

Have you cloth or not? = *Nī scü lilīlā?*

I have much cloth = *Aiyo ōscü elam līā.*

Bring my book which is on the table = *Ā kāko pīlang līānāchī hānsī yīā.*

The word for "is" is often omitted: *e.g.*—

He is my brother = { *Shīcho ā tā.* / *Ātā shī.* / *Ātācho shī.* }

This is good, that is bad = *Shīcho mhōnā, chicho m-mho.*

I am eating = *Ānā tsōālā.*

I am sleeping = *Ānā yipālā.*

The form of this verb is generally *cho* in the past tense and *chākā* in the present perfect and pluperfect tenses:—

I ate = *Ānā tsōcho.*

Lit.—I eating was.

I have eaten all = *Ānā tsōchākā.*

The affix *lā* is frequently retained in the past tenses.

(*b*) "Be," "have" in the sense of continuing is expressed by the verb *vānā* = "stay,", "remain," "inhabit," &c:—

Have you a wife? = *Ni eng vāvānilā?*

Is the Sahab in? = *Etsi tāçhūngi vāvānilā?*

He is not in { *N-vān.* / *M-mā.* }

He was here yesterday = *Nchö hinā hello vāncho.*

ADVERBS, ADVERBIAL PHRASES, AND AFFIXES.

Adverbs of Time.

After a little = *Ōkhaicho esangāro vāsi, terrārovasi, okhānāti.*

Afternoon = *Nyūlāni.*

Afterwards = *Hisi, thāmpōlhang, thāmphōthang.*

After a few days = *Nchōk enni etham vāsu, nchōk mezu mūngo vāsu.*

A while ago = *Vangā, nthongnā.*

Again = *Ennōā.*—Verbal affix *lān* (see Illustrative Sentences).

Ago, long since = *Nkōlō.*

Always = *Echūng, nchünkō.*

Before = *Vangā,* long before = *nkōlō* (see Illustrative Sentences for negative with participles of time).

By day = *Engilo.*

By night = *Zamōlo.*

Cock-crow = *Hōno khūāthang.*

Constantly = / Continually = / Habitually = / Unceasingly = } Verbal affixes *khangā* and *pvū.*

Daily = *Nchōnthang n̈chōnthang, nchōk-nchōkā.*

Dusk (at) = *Mangsāthang.*

Evening (in the) = *Mangchōlo.*

First = verbal affix *ten* (see Illustrative Sentences), *vangā.*

Formerly = *Ōsinā.*

Frequently = *Nsānsām.*

Henceforth = *Hisicho.*

Last night = *Nsamo.*

Last year = *Lānkamo.*

Last month = *Chōro tchīchākā.*

Late—*Nshuthangā.*

Month (this) = *Chōro sḥi.*

Month (next) = *Chōro ōpōmwe.*

Never = *Kōthanghā*, followed by a negative.

Night (by) = *Zamōlo.*

Night before last = *Ōchyū zamō.*

Nightly = *Zamōthang zamōthang. Zamolo zamōlo.*

Noon (at) = *Nshi ethango.*

Now = *Nthāngā.*

Now-a-days = *Nchaiyā hichō.*

Now and then = *Kōthanghā kōthanghā.*

Often = *N-sāṉnsām.*

One day = *Tsangōnā, engyā, nchōkā.*

One night = *Zamōā.*

Quickly = *Nthāṉgā, ekhiolakā, setōā, ndrā.*

Regularly—adverbial affix *pheṉphenochi.*

Sometimes = *Kōthanghā kōthanghā.*

Soon = *Ōkhānāti, sangāro vāsu.*

Suddenly = *Ekhiāpā.*

Sunrise = *Engi chirōpānthang.*

Sunset = *Engi threpānthango.*

The day before yesterday = *Zamcho.*

The day after tomorrow = *Rāchō.*

To-day = *Nching.*

To-night = *Ōsamo.*

Tomorrow = *Ōchō.*

Until—(See Illustrative Sentences.)

While—affixes *thang* and *le.* (See Illustrative Sentences.)

When = *Kōthang*, and *thang*, the particle of time, with the verb.

Adverbs of Manner.

Accidentally = *N-tsühā, m-mhung.*

Along (in company with) = *Pānā, nzo, süerā.*

Alone = *Ōmōti.*

Also = *Hā.*

Badly = *M-mhō, yüsōrā.*

Designedly = *Ntsiāhā.*

Equally = *Khiti khiti, keli keti.*

Gently = *Ennānātō.*

How = *Kōtōli, kōtō.*

Immediately = *Nthāngā, ndrā.*

In this way = *Hetō.*

In that way = *Chitō.*

In what way = *Kōtüv.*

Loudly = *Ekhiotō.*

More = *Sā* (verbal affix), *ennōā.*

No = *Me, mek.*

Perhaps = *Kānyü.*

Probably = *Esā, kāche.*

Quickly = } *Ekhiāpā, ekhiōlā*
Rapidly = } *ndrā, setōā.*

Silently = *Mphōā, ethak n-tsyü, ennāto.*

Slightly = *Etchukāro, terrāro.*

Slowly = *Echamchamnā.*

Tightly = *Rōk rōk, rak rak, tā nangā, rārangā.*

Truly = *Ōtscōtcō.*

Very well = *Nnānyū.*

Well = *Mhōna.*

Wholly = *Kān* (verbal affix.)

Why = *Ntsōle, nyūwōtsōle.*

Yes = *Hō.*

ADVERBS OF PLACE.

Above = *Ōpōni,* affix, *ō* or *lō, ōyāki, omhauwe.*

Afar (from) = *Ekōninā.*

Afar (off) = *Ekōni.*

Ahead = *Ōvangwe, ōvangi.*

Anywhere = *Kūwesanā, kūsānā, kūisānā.*

Around = *Hriphiā, kāfūā.*

At a short distance = *Nhyankhang.*

At some distance = *Nkōnkhang.*

At the right hand = *Āmymwe.*

At the left hand = *Aiyiwe.*

Back side = *Silāmwe, ōchūwe* (of bed). *Khantsangwe* (of house).

Backwards = *Silāmphiwō.*

Behind = *Silāmwe.*

Below = *Ōkhapwe, ndrewe, ōkhapi.*

Beside = *Tsātsōkwe*

Elsewhere = *Thāmphōe.*

Everywhere = *Metā ākūā, metā ākwai, metātshū, metā meyo.*

From above = *Ōyākinā.*

From below = *Ōkapinā.*

From within = *Ōchūngwenā, tāchūngwenā.*

From without = *Hōmphōwenā.*

Hence = *Hellonā, hepinā.*

Here = *Hello, shilo, hepi.*

High = *Ōyāki.*

Hither = *Épi, hepi, hello.*

In front = *Thōnthryūwe.*

Inside = *Tāchūngwe, takuwe.*

In the presence of = *Mhātūngwe.*

In the middle = *Ōnūngo.*

Near = *Enghyāno.*

On this side = *Hepiwe, hepōmwe, epōmwe.*

On that side = *Ōchiwe, ōpōmwe.*

Somewhere = *Kūsānā, kūlōsānā.*

Thence = *Ōchinā.*

There = *Ōchi-ōchilo.*

Whence = *Kūinā, kūnā, kūlonā.*

Whither = *Kūi.*

ILLUSTRATIVE SENTENCES.

Come again = *Ennōā rōā.* / *Ennōā rōkenā.* / *Rōlānā.*

Eat before you go = *N-yithanghā tsōā.*

Lit.—Not going time eat.

He cries constantly = *Hinā kiāpvū kiāpvu vānālā.*

He is habitually cross = *Hicho lam tscokhāngā.*

I came first = { *Ānā rōtencho.*
Ānā ōvanginā rōcho. }

He comes regularly at noon = *Nshuthangāthang ōmō rōphen rōpheno rōālā.*

Stay here until I return = *Ānā n-rōlānthango hello vānā.*

I can't go while he is here = *Hi hello vānāthang ānā m-mōkōk.*

I saw a tiger while going along the road = *Ānā ōlani wōle mhorr mhūngcho.*

Give me more = *A pisā.*

Very well, I'll go if you like = *Nnānyū, ānā wōkhānyū.*

He sleeps at the back-side, I sleep at the front-side = *Hinā ōchūwe yip ānā ōmiwe yip.*

POSTPOSITIONS.

In Lhōtā, as in other Nāgā languages, the words identical in power with the English prepositions follow the words which they govern, and hence are called postpositions. The following are some of these words with their ordinary significations. See also case terminations under nouns, where the affixes here mentioned are illustrated :—

Above = *Ōmhai, ōmhainā, ōmhauwe.*

After = *Silāmi* (along with), *pānā.*

Among = *Ōnūngo.*

As far as = *Te hngā, ntānte.*

At, in = Affix *lo, nā, thang.*

Before = *Ōvangwe, ōvangi.*

,, (to the presence of) = *Mhātanginā.*

,, (in the presence of) = *Mhātangi, tonthryūwe.*

Below = *Ōkapi, ōkapwe, ōkhapwe.*

Beside = *Tsātsōkwe.*

Between = *Yite, ōnūngi.*

Beyond = *Engamwe.*

By = Affix *nā.*

For = *Etsōnā, etchū, etchi,* affix *lō, ō* and *kiattō.*

From = *Theni,* affix *nā.*

In, into = *Tāchūngi, ōchūngwe,* affix *i.*

In place of = *Nniche.*

In the direction of = Affix *we.*

On, unto, upon—*Ōpōni,* affixes *ō, lō, ōlō, we.*

To—*Sheni thingi, themwe,* affix *i, lō.*

Toward, at—*Themwe,* affix *we.*

With—*Pānā, nzo, sirrā, theni.*

Thang often governs a verb or participle in the sense of while:—*e.g.*—

While staying at Wokha I was ill.
Wōke vānāthang ā pīrapthātā.

Come in the morning.
Engīyāthang rōā.
Lit.—Sun coming time come.

The following are a few examples of the use of other postpositions:—

The birds fly above our heads=*Ā kurr mhainā wōro phyai īyā.*

Come after me=*Ā silamī rōa.*

Come along with me=*Ā pānā rōā.*

He lives among us=*Hinā enūngo vānā.*

Go as far as the bazaar=*Bōzārelo n-tānte wōā.*

Come as far as the tree=*Ōtōng he te hngā iyā.*

I bought this of your brother=*Nitā theni shī shicho.*

Go towards the Sahab's house=*Etsi kiwe wōā.*

Throw that toward the tree=*Ōtōngchi themwe shamchiā.*

Go between the houses=*Ōkī yitenā wōā.*

He sleeps between us=*Hinā enī nūngī yipālā.*

CONJUNCTIONS.

Lhōtā Nāgā, like the other languages of this type, abounds in participial expressions, a structure not favourable to the use of connectives. See under Participles.

The following are the most common connectives:—

And=*Nā, hā, sū, nnā.*

And (more)=*Sü.*

Also=*Hā.*

Both—and=*Hā-hā.*

But=*Tōsü, ōsü, sü, tōlehā.*

If=*nā.*

If not=*menā.*

Then / Thereupon }=*Chisicho.*

Therefore=*Chitsakōnā, chī etscakōnā.*

ILLUSTRATIVE SENTENCES.

The following sentences will illustrate the use of the conjunctions, and also how their place is supplied by conjunctive participles:—

The Sahab, the Babu, and I will go=*Etsi nā Babu nā ā tō wō.*

Etsihā Babu hā ānā ha tō ethamātō wō.

Both he and I will go.= { *Shinā ā tō wō.*
Shi hā ānā hā tō wō.

The Sahab's pony is dead and mine also=*Etsi korr tchü nā ā korr ha tchü.*

One rupee and two annas=*Piākā sü mōiyā.*

A hundred and more besides=*Nzoā sü enōā chi ḥā liā.*

Go and eat =*Ōyi tsōā.*

Lit.—Going eat.

I went to Wokha and bought fowls=*Ānā Wōkhe wōsi hōno sicho.*

Lit.—I Wokha having gone fowls bought.

Although you go I will not come=*Nnā wōlehā aiyo ndrō.*

Lit.—You although going I will not come.

Although I went I did not see any one=*Ānā wōā hā ōyāṉ m-mhūng.*

Lit.—I although going another person saw not.

I cannot go because I am sick=*Ā pirapthākamā aiyō m-mōkōk.*

Lit.—I ill being I cannot go.

I cannot eat more now for I am full=*Nthāngā ā nhyichā kamā nthāngo n-tsōkōk.*

Lit.—Now I full being more cannot eat.

Give me this, but if not, give me that=*Shi ā piā, osü menā, chi ā piā.*

Lit.—This me give, but, if not, that me give.

Go, but don't stay long = *Wōā, ōsi enhyākā ti vānā.*

Lit.—Go, but long don't stay.

Either you or he come tomorrow = *Ōchō nnā n-rōnā hinā rōā.*

Lit.—To morrow you not coming he come.

Neither you nor he must come = *Nnā hā tī rōā nā shīhā tī rōā.*

Lit.—You also not come and he also not come.

Except this there is no other = *Shī te kamā thāmphō n-nī.*

Lit.—This only being other not.

If you go, don't stay long = *Nnā wōnā enhyākā ti vānā.*

Lit.—You if going long don't stay.

I will not go *lest* it may rain = *Erū chō esā kamā aiyō m-mo.*

Lit.—Rain perhaps being I will not go.

I am doing this well in order that the Sahab may give me a present = *Etsīnā ōthān ā pitōkūkīattō ānā shi mhōnā lyūālā.*

This is bad, nevertheless I'll eat it = *Shīchō m-mhōlā, tòlā ānā tsō kānyū.*

You come or else send Nymstsemo = *Nnō rōā, ōsū, menā, Nymtsemō rōtōkā.*

Lit.—You come, but, if not, Nymtsemo cause to come.

If you go then I will not go=*Nnā wōnā chinā aiyō m-mō.*

Lit.—You if going, on that I will not go.

Having done my work I then went to the bazaar=*Ānā nsūndryūsi chisicho bāzāre chōwōcho.*

Lit.—I work having done then (after that) to the bazaar went.

He has gone therefore I will not go=*Shīnā wōcho ānā chītscūkōnā m-mō.*

Lit.—He has gone I for this will not go.

We cannot go unless both go=*Nī nā ā tō menā m-mōkōk.*

Lit.—You and I if not cannot go.

I cannot go unless you go=*Nnā maknā ānā m-mōkōk.*

Lit.—You if not I cannot go.

My father has gone and so I did not go = *Āpōnā ichā kamā ānā chi etscōnā m-mōcho.*

Lit.—My father having gone I for this cause did not go.

INTERJECTIONS.

Admiration = *Āpāpā, aiyo, aiyo.*

Annoyance = *Eṉeṉ, haiyo-o.*

Approval—bravo, bravo = *Hāhā, monsonto monsonto.*

Assent—yes = *Hō.*

Yes, yes = *Hō, hō.*

To attract attention = *Hai, hai,* the reply *hō, hāṉ.*

To attract attention to one's words = *Ntātō.*

Disgust = *Eṉ, eṉ. Āṉhāṉh.* (Violent spitting generally accompanies these exclamations.)

Sorrow = *Hāpvo hāpvo, hāpvo-ā.*

TABLES.

Money Table.

Rāngmyō terrūwō = 1 pie.
Lit.—Money red small.

Rāngmyō matsangā = 1 pice.
Lit.—Money red one.

Rāngmyō enni = 2 pice.
Lit.—Money red two.

Rāngmyō etham = 3 pice.
Lit.—Money red three.

Rāngmyō mezü = 4 pice.
Lit.—Money red four., &c.

Rāng terru e-hm = 2 annas.
Lit.—Money small white.

Mōiyā is now a more common term for 2 annas

Rāmpiāk pōko or rāngmyō tizā = 8 annas.
Lit.—Rupee half *or* money red eight.

Rāmpiāk = 1 rupee.

The Lhōtās now generally use the word *poisā* for pice, counting thus—

Poisā matsangā, poisā enni, etc.

Moiyā matsangā, moiyā enni, etc.

{ *Ōrāng* / *Rampiāk* } *matsangā*, { *Ōrāng* / *Rumpiak* } *enni*, &c.

Space Measurement.

Ekō = a span.

Eko hendlo = a span with forefinger.

Eko sappō = a span with middle finger.

Khechū = a cubit.

Wōnchen̲ = an arm's length.

Nki = distance covered by both arms extended.

Mungyā = distance from breast bone to finger's end.

Chōhmyekchānchākā = ankle-high (spoken of water and growing grains).

Ndrā ekhangchānchākā = half the height to the knee.

Nko chānchākā = knee high.

Phinang chānchākā = thigh-high.

Kangke chānchākā = leg-high.

Eryū chānchākā = waist-high.

Khōyo chānchākā = rib-high.

Ōhiro chanchakā = breast-high.

Distances are estimated by the time it takes to accomplish them.

Nchōkā etsā = one day's journey = 40 to 50 miles.

Nchōk enni etsā = two days' journey.

Capacity.

Myōkū pyangā, *Myō esānā* } = one handful.

Okhe tsongkōn̲ pyangā, *Nchamā* } = two handfuls.

Basket Measures.

Tsangtsirō, *Tsangthephen̲* } = about 2 chuttacks.

Lōtāng, *Lālōn̲* } = about 1 powah.

Rammā = about 2 powahs.

Etakā = about 1 seer.

Lekham = 4 to 5 seers.

Efū=a small balance for weighing salt and meat. Will weigh up to 4 or 5 seers.

TIME.

Divisions of Day and Night.

A day=*Nchōkā* / *Tsangngōnā* } =24 hours.

A day=*Engā*=one sun.

Daytime=*Nchōnthang.*

Before cock-crow=*Hōnō khūsāthang.*

Cock-crow=*Hōnō khūāthang.*

Early morning= { *Nyāzanginā.* / *Nyāpā.*

Sunrise=*Engiyāthang*=sun-coming time.

Morning=*Eng chiropān thang.*

Forenoon=*Eng langhi chūngrōchākā.*

Mid-day=*Nshiethango*=luncheon time.

Afternoon=*Nyūlāni.*

After lunch follow three drinking times, which serve to divide the afternoon into the three following parts:—

Sendro lānghauwō.
Sendro ōnnūgo.
Sendro lānkupō.

Late afternoon= { *Engi hrepangō* / *Engi hrepsāthang.* } = sun descending time.

Dusk= { *Mangsāthang* / *Mangpanthang* } = dark getting time.

Sunset= { *Engi hrepānthang.* / *Engi hrechākchōlo.*

Night=*Zamō.*

Midnight= { *Zamō nangten.* / *Zamō chyūsōe.*

Divisions of Month.

The moon / A month } =*Chōro.*

New moon= { *Chōro pānthang.* / *Chōro chiropānthang.*

Half moon=*Chōro ekavsā.*

Full moon = *Chōro ekālā.*

Time between moons = *Chōram.*

The moon is waxing = *Chōro rānchetālā.*

The moon is waning = *Chōro zākātā iyālā.*

The moon is about to die = *Choro tchyūvsālā.*

The moon has died
The month has closed } = *Chōro tchichākā.*

Months.

January = *Etsōn, Echōn.*
February = *Ndri.*
March = *Emhū* = "to blow," as in lighting a fire and refers to the firing of jungle on the cultivations.
April = *Ephi.*
May = *Chesu.*
June = *Eten,* from *oten* = "Kōni dhan."
July = *Nnung.*
August = *Chikānikā.*
September = *Ndrang.*
October = *Chōchāntsu.*
November = *Rongorongyi* referring to the passing and repassing in carrying the "dhan" from the fields to the village.
December = *Puthe hānte* = Crop.

Seasons.

Hot weater = *Elamō.*
Cold weather = *Etsakō.*
Sowing time = *Yichenthang, līchenthang.*
Before harvest = *Yīrapang, līchenthang.*
Harvest time = *Yīrāthang, lirāthang.*
Rest time = *Mānü thang.*
Rains = *Nsūlo.*

SYNTAX.

Owing to the frequent omission of subject nominatives, the preponderance of participial expressions, and an indifferent system of inflections, syntax plays a very important part in the construction of the Lhōtā Nāgā language.

(*1*) *Order of words in a simple sentence.*

The verb stands last in the sentence, and, as a rule, the subject stands first. Considerable freedom, however, is allowed as regards the position of the latter. It is frequently omitted, and any nouns or pronouns standing in a possessive relation to it always precede it.

Adverbs often take the first place in a sentence.

Interrogative adverbs, however, take this place less often than in English.

He struck me=*Hinā ā tāpcho.*
Lit.—He me struck.

My father struck him=*Á pōnā shī tāpcho.*
Lit.—My father him struck.

When did he strike you?=*Shīnā kōthang ni tāpchōlā?*
Lit.—He when you struck?

He struck me yesterday=*Nchö hinā ā tāpcho.*
Lit.—Yesterday he me struck.

Adjectives follow the nouns they qualify. In case, however, the relation of the qualifying adjective is so intimate as to form with the noun a compound word it precedes the latter: *e.g.*—

An Assamese man=*Ōsam kyōn.*

The articles *nchyūā, matsangā, ntsangā, hi, shi,* and *chi* follow the nouns which they define—

A (one) horse=*Korr matsangā.*

The (this) dog=*Phūrro shi.*

When both the article and an adjective qualify a noun, the article follows the adjective—

A (one) white horse=*Korr ehem matsangā.*

The (that) beautiful girl=*Lōrōroe mhōm chi.*

Possessive nouns and pronouns precede the name of the object possessed:

My house=*Á ki.*

Nymtsemō's father=*Nymtsemō ōpō.*

Adverbs frequently stand first in a sentence—

He came yesterday=*Nchö hinā rōcho.*

Adverbs qualifying adjectives or other adverbs immediately precede them—

He is very sick= { *Hi tangto pirapthātā,*
Hi elam pirapthātā. }

He came very quickly=*Hi tangtō ekhyangā yiā.*

The verbal affixes *lān, sā, pvū,* &c., having the force of adverbs follow the verbal root—

Come back again=*Rōlānā.*

Give me more=*Ā pisā.*

He comes frequently=*Hi rōpvū rōpvū vānālā.*

Adverbs qualifying a whole clause precede or follow the subject indifferently :—

I never spoke with him= { *Ānā kōthanghā shi n-chā.* / *Kōthanghā ānā shi n-chā.* }

(2) *Position of clauses in a sentence.*

In complex sentences the principal clause stands last, and relative clauses, and constructions taking their place, precede antecedent clauses :—

Go and tell John what you have seen and heard.

Nnā ntiō ntiō mhūng, ntiō ntio zo, chī wōsi Yōhān ezoā.

Lit.—What you have seen, what heard, that having gone, to John tell.

Where did he tell you that the pony was ?

Shinā korrchb kū vāncho lāto, ni zōchōlā ?

Lit.—He pony where was saying you told ?

I know that a goat is there.

Chī nyānyā vānā, ānā ntsū.

On this principle verbal adjectives precede the nouns they qualify :—

He killed all who were staying in the house here.

Ōki chilo evān lāngā henā nangthāta.

Lit.—House here in staying all he killed.

For the construction of participial clauses, see explanations under Participles and Conjunctions.

Interrogative and negative constructions are sufficiently explained under verbs.

(3) *Direct and indirect quotations.*

Direct quotations are immediately followed by the particle *tō* and are generally placed between the subject and predicate of the principal clause:—

He says I will go=*Shinā "ānā wō" tō phyōālā.*

Lit.—He "I will go" says.

He said to me I am sick=*Hinā "a pirāpthātā" tō ezōchō.*

When thoughts are expressed in any other form than in the original words of the author, the affix *làtō* is employed at the close of the indirect discourse which, as a rule, follows the principal clause :—

He says that he would go = *Hinā phyōālā, ōmōnā wōlàtō.*
He told me that he was sick = *Hinā ā zōcho, ōmō pirapthelato.*

If the speaker says "*Ānā wō*"="I will go," any one standing near and wishing to inform a third party of the fact, will simply say "*Wōlatō*" = "He says that he will go."

PHRASES ILLUSTRATING THE USE OF VERBS.

INDICATIVE MOOD.

Present Tense.

Ache, root = *Nō*.

1. Does your head *ache* now-a-days?	*Epaiyācho ni kurr ni nōtātānüng ?* *Epaiyācho ni kurr ni nōtāchōke ?*
2. Yes, it *aches* . . .	*Ho, ā nōā.* *Ho, ā nōtātā.* *Ho, ā nōtsangā.*
3. Does it *ache* much ? . . 4. Yes, it *aches* hard . .	*Elam ni nōāke ?* *Ho, tangto ā nōā.* *Ho, mpemo ā nōā.*

Ask, root = *Ngā*.

5. Do you *ask* the Sahab whether you can *go* or not ?	*Nnā wōālo m-mōsānā etsi engālānung ?*
6. I do not *ask* him . .	*Ānā hi n-gā.*
7. Do you *ask* the Sahab or not ?	*Nno etsi ngāngêlā ?*
8. Yes, I *ask* him now and then	*Ho, kōthanghā, kothanghā ānā shi engā.*

Assemble, root = *tscō*, with *nzo* or *kōlōk:*

9. Do you *cause* the coolies to *assemble ?*	*Nno kūli kōlōk tscōyitokānung ?*
10. No, they *assemble* themselves.	*Me, ōmōmō nzō tscōyiālā.*

Present Imperfect.

Beat, root = *tāp*.

11. Is he *beating* you? . .	*Hinā ni tāpālānung?*
12. Yes, he is continually *beating* me.	*Ho, hinā ā tāpvūvānālā.* *Ho, hinā ā tāpkangā.*
13. Why is he *beating* you? .	*Ntsōle hinā ni tāpālā?*
14. I struck him first and so he is now *beating* me.	*Ānā hi tāptencho ole ōmōnā nthāngā ā tāpālā.*
15. I am not *beating* him now .	*Nthāngā ānā hi tāpā m-mānāha.*
16. When I *struck* him a while ago I did not *get* a chance to *beat* him, so I am *beating* him now.	*Ōmōnā nthōng ā tāple ānā ōmō n-tāphrākhamā, nthāngā hi-tāpālā.*

Blow, root = *ve*.

17. The wind *is blowing* . .	*Mpōng vênālā.*
18. Now it is not *blowing* .	*Nthāngā m-me.* *Nthāngā n-ve.*

Blow, root = *Mhū*.

19. Why does the boy *keep blowing* the fire?	*Nyūtsōle nungōrnā ōmi mhūāvānālā?*
20. I am *making him* blow it .	*Anā hi hmtōkālā.* *Ānā hi mhūtōkālā.*

Blow, root = *Sā*.

21. Is there a breeze *blowing* or not?	*Züro sāsāpālā?*
22. A slight breeze *is blowing* .	*Züro terrāro esāpālā.*

Past Imperfect.

Boil, roots = *lā* and *she*.

23. When you *came* was the water *boiling*?	*Nno yiathang ōtchhü elākālanüng?* *Nno yiathang ōtchhü shenānüng?*
24. It was not *boiling* . .	*Elākā m-mā.* *Shenā m-mā.*
25. It was *boiling* an hour .	*Shālā matsangā elākāvāncho.* *Shālā matsangā shenāvanā.*

Past Tense.

Borrow, root = *No.*

26. Yesterday I *borrowed* ten rupees of the Babu. — *Nchö ānā bābū theni oràng tāro nōcho.*

27. I did not *borrow* anything of him. — *Ānā hi theni nyūhā n-no.*
Ānā hī theni nyūhā n-nōcho.

Break, root = *Khirap.*

28. Did you *break* this dish? . — *Nno ōpfhū hi khirapchōke?*

29. I did not *break* it . . — *Anā hī n-khirap.*

30. When I was holding it in my hand my brother, knocking it out of my hand, *broke* it. — *Anā peṉle ā tānā ewōnchōchī khirapcho.*

31. He made me *break* it . — *Hinā shi ā khiraptōkcho.*

Present Perfect.

Break, root = *vāso.*

32. Have you *broken* the stones? — *Nno ōnūng vāsōchākānüng?*

33. I have not *broken* them all . — *Ānā ōmpā m-māsōāhā.*

Break, root = *rānso.*

34. Have you *broken* my spear or not? — *Ā tso erānsōçhākchōālo n-rānsōāhālā?*

35. I have made my brother *break* it. — *Ānā hi ātā erānsōlōkchākā.*

Past Perfect.

Burn, root = *rōng.*

36. They themselves had *burned* their village before we arrived. — *Enā wō n-chanthangā ōmōchihā ōyān rōngchākā* or *rōngā.*

Bring, root = *hāṉ yi.*

37. When you were there, had he *brought* the fowls? — *Nnā ōchi vānāthang hinā hōnō hāṉsi yichākānüng?*

38. He had not *brought* the fowls, but he had brought the eggs. — *Shinā kōnocho hāṉsi n-yinī hōno tchhü hānsi yichākā.*

Future Tense.

Build, root = *Tscō.*

39. I *will build* a house . .	*Ānā ōki tscō.*
40. Where will you *build* it? .	*Nno kūwe tscōlā?*
41. Will they *let* you *build* here?	*Ōnō hello nī tscōlōkūla?*
42. Yes, they *will let* me *build* here.	*Ho, hello ā tscōtōku khānyū.*
43. I am about *to build* a house.	*Ānā ōki tsōvsā.* *Ānā ōki tsōvsākhāmā.*
44. Will you *build* a large house or a small one?	*Nno ōki tsapō tscōālo etchukāro tscōālā?*
45. Will you *build* at once?	*Nthāngā tscōānung?* *Nthāngā tscōke?*

Imperative Mood.

Call, root = *Tsā.*

46. *Call* the messenger . .	*Lāmpen̲ tsā.*
47. *Don't call* him now, *call* him afterwards.	*Nthānga tī tsā, ōkhānāti tsā.*
48. *Don't let* him *call* loudly .	*Ekhyo tī tsātōkā.*

Potential Mood.

Capture, root = *Hram.*

49. We *cannot capture* the thief	*Enā efūcho n-hramākōk.*
50. We *can catch* him tomorrow	*Ōchō enā hi hramākōkū.* *Ōchō enā hi hramākōkū kānyū.*

Carry, root = *Hān.*

51. As I was ill yesterday, I could not *carry* my burden.	*Nchō ā phīraptākhāmā ānā ā hān̲ m-hānkōk.*

Carry, root = *Pū.*

52. I could not *make* him *carry* me.	*Ānā shi ā pūtōkletō n-tōkū.*
53. Can you *make* him *carry* the sick man?	*Nnā phīraptāwōchinā shi khī pūtōkōkūnūng?*

Climb = *Chūngwā.*

54. May I *climb* this tree?	*Ōtōng shi ānā chūngwāne?*
55. Yes, if you wish you may *climb* it.	*Ho, ni chungwōhngnā chūngnōnā te khānyu.*

SUBJUNCTIVE MOOD.

56. Catch the cat quickly, she may *climb* the tree.	*Ōlyuro ōlōngi chūngyiū escükā ekiāpā hramātā.*
57. He may *close* the door	*Hinā hānkhāṉ khāmū escā.*

Lit.—He door will close perhaps.

Collect (revenue), root = *khī.*

58. If you had *collected* the revenue, I would have *given* you one hundred rupees.	*Nnā lōkotsen khīāwō ōrang nzoa ni piūkàtōlā.*

Collect, root = *tscō.*

59. If you will *collect* (assemble) the coolies, I will *pay* them.	*Nno kūlī kōlōk, tscōitōknā chitosati ōtscen pīyū.*

Cluck, root = *kōkā.*

60. I do not *know* whether the hen *clucks* or not.	*Hōnōnā kōkōkākānā ānā n-tsü.*

Passive Voice.

Command, root = *pangnōā.*

61. I have been *commanded* to go.	*Wōleto ā pangnochākā.*

Complete, root = *metā.*

62. The work has been *completed* four days.	*Nchōk mezü nsundnyukāmā metākchākā.*

NEUTER VERBS.

63. I *am* cold	*Ā-tsaktsangā.* *Ā-tsakālā.* *Ā tsaktālā.* *Ā tsakā.*
64. I *was* cold 65. I *have been* cold	*Ā tsaktsangā.* *Ā tsakā.* *Ā tsaktātā.*

66. If it is cold I will not go .	*Etsaknā ānā m-mō.*
67. Although I am tired I will go	*Āmōktsanglehā ānā wō.*

Also see under Predicate Adjectives.

For illustrations of Infinitive, Supine, Participles, and verbal modifiers, see under these respective heads in the discussion of the verbs. See also under Conjunctions.

PHRASES ILLUSTRATING THE USE OF THE DIFFERENT PARTS OF SPEECH.

1. I see *a* man *and* a horse .	*Ānā kyōn̲ nā korr tō mhüngālā* (No article expressed.)

Ana kyōn̲ nchyūā *na korr* matsangā *tō mhüngālā.*

Lit.—I man one and horse one see.

2. *A* goat's horn . . .	*Nyānyā etchhü.*
3. For carrying burdens for the sepoys over to Themokudima Nāgās get eight annas *a* day.	*Kyōnā sepe hān̲ hān̲si Chemāngi thrōwōnā engā lōnā ādhōli piālā.*
4. Yesterday *a* (one) man came here.	*Nchö kyōn̲* nchyūā *ēpi rōcho.*
5. I will remain here *about* a year.	*Ānā hēlo nzü mātsāngā* hākōno *vām.*
6. What is he *about?* . .	*Hicho ntīwo lyūālā?*
7. I went all *about* your village .	*Ānā ni yānī etchiyūā kiācho ezīyūā.*
8. Nāgās stood *about* the Sahib	*Kiōnā etsi* hāchammī *vāncho.*
9. What are you talking *about?*	*Nno nyūnō chāntālā.*
10. We are talking *about* going to Lungsai.	*Enā Lūngse chōwō chāntālā.*
11. The calf appears *about* to die	*Māngsü rōchi tchhyū* sālā.
12. Birds fly *above* our heads .	*Wōrōnā e kurrī*ụā *pyā yiālā.*
13. *Above* this sky there is also another.	*Potsōwo shī* mhai *enūngāhā potsōwo liyelātō.*
14. Wokha is *above* Yikụm village	*Wōkhaicho yikam yān̲* mhai.
15. Give me the book which is *above*, *i.e.* on top.	Opōni *evan̲wō kāko chī ā piā.*
16. How many days has Lentie been *absent?*	*Lentiōnā yisī nchōk kōtā wōlā?*

Lit.—Lentie having gone days how many gone.

17. He has been *absent* two days	*Shinā yisī nchōk eni wō.*
18. He *abuses* me . . .	*Shinā ā* mākālā.
19. Keep an accurate *account* .	*Ōtscōtscō* kai *vātā.*

20. My head *aches* . . .	*Ā kurrinā ā* nōālā.
21. I am a man from *across* the river.	*Aio pōfū nā* pānkauwe *kyōṉ.*
22. A tree has fallen *across* the road.	*Ōtōng eyai ōlāṉ eyāzā.*
23. Creep *across* on the tree .	*Ōtōngo yāngkātā yāngkātā iyā.*
24. Cutting a tree and putting it *across* come over.	*Ōtōng tāni rōkai ezā iya.*
25. The water being deep I cannot go *across* on foot.	*Ōtchhü chungwākammā ānā n'-khingkākōk.*
26. If you tell the truth it will be to your *advantage.*	*Ninā ōtscōtscō phyōnā ni etchi* kākcho.
27. Seeing an orange tree *afar* off he went to it.	*Shinā kōngke tōng* ekōnī *mhung-chi wōcho.*
28. Are you *afraid?* . .	*Ni* khyūāke?
29. Don't be *afraid* . . .	*Ti* khyūā.
30. I am not *afraid* . . .	*Ā* n'khen.
31. I am *afraid* . . .	*A* khenālā, (*or*) *Ā* khentsangā.
32. *After* he had gone I arrived	*Shinā yi*tōnā *ānā chhānto.*
33 Don't tell me now, tell me *afterwards.*	*Nthāngācho a ti zoā,* ōkhānātī *ā zoā.*
34. Come *after* (along with) me .	*Ā* pānā *rōā.*
35. He is coming *after* (behind) me.	*Shinā ā* sīlāmwe *iyālā.*
36. *Afterwards* the boys will know their books. (By and by, before long.)	Ōkhaicho *nūngōrishiangnā kāko ntsiyū.*
37. *After* a long time I shall go .	Ōkhcletī *ānā wō.*
38. I'll go *after* a little . .	*Ānā* ōkhānātī *wō.*
39. *After* a while the Sahib will go over to Kohima.	*Etsinā* hīsī *Kōhime thrōwō.*
40. *After* having presented the Sahib with a fowl, he will decide the matter.	*Etsī hōnō kūbsānāti chitōsānāti ōyilo ethiū.*
41. Come *after* you have eaten your rice.	*Otsī tsōs*ī *rōā.*
42. *Afterwards* (at another time) I'll buy a cow.	Tāmpōthung *ānā māngsū shiyū.*
43. I will come again in the *afternoon.*	*Ānā eng* ehrelānī *yilām.*
44. Don't come *again* . .	Enūngo *ti rōā,* (or) *Ti rō*lānā.
45. Listen, he speaks *again* .	*Shinā* enīwōhā *phyōj etākā, ungā.*

46.	He is leaning *against* the tree	*Ōtōngi* engōke *vānālā.*
47.	Will you come *again* or not?	*Nō* nthāngo *rōrōlā?*
48.	I will not come *again* . .	*Āio n'rō*lām.
49.	Don't throw stones *against* the house.	*Ōnūng ki ōki ti ephiā*kātā.
50.	He ran *against* the fence .	*Shīnā pāhrilo chen*kācho.
51.	He is leaning *against* the tree	*Ōtōngi* engōke *vānālā.*
52.	He is speaking *against* you .	*Shinā ni etchak etchi rālā.*
53.	He is *against* me . .	*Shi ā yātāpen.*
54.	What is your *age?* . .	*Nno* nzu kōtā wê lā? (*or*) wō lā? *Ni* pōksī nzu kōtāu lā?
55.	I am twelve years of *age* .	*Āio nzu tārō si enī wō.* *Āio ā pōksu nzu tāro si enī pentākā.*
56.	He is very *aged* . . .	*Shicho elum* scōntsungā.
57.	He died six months *ago* .	*Shī tchhisi chōro tirōk* tsōtākā.
58.	This house was built long *ago*	Nkōlōnā *ōki shi tsōtākā.* (or) *Ōki shi tsōsī* elum sungtākā.
59.	Very, very long *ago* tigers married men.	Nkōlō mutsinā *mhurrnā kiōn̲ sōāvāncho.*
60.	He went a little while *ago* .	*Shicho* ntōngnā *yicho.*
61.	He went a few (4 or 5) days *ago.*	*Nchōk mezu mungālo īyā.*
62.	He went some time *ago* .	*Shicho* ōsinā *yicho.*
63.	The boat is *aground* . .	*Ōhrōng* chūngte *tālā.*
64.	He has gone on *ahead* . .	*Shī* ōvungīnā *yitākā.*
65.	Wait I'll go *ahead* of you (before).	*Ōsā ānā ni* vungī *wō.*
66.	I will go *ahead* (in front) of you.	*Ānā ni* mhātūngī *wō.*
67.	*Alas* my dhân is all destroyed	Haiyōn *a tsōk hetōpū eshōkānī siā.*
68.	These two are *alike* (exactly alike).	*Shī ōni* kitī.
69.	Are *all* the boys here? .	*Nūngōr* hetōpū *hello vān̲vān̲nīlā?* (or) *vān̲vān̲drelā?*
70.	Has *all* the cloth been brought in?	*Ōscū* hālāngtō *hān̲sī threitākchō-ālo?*
71.	*All* men must die . .	*Kiōn̲*tzu *tchhikam.*
72.	*All* Angami land . .	*Tsungōn̲ metā*tzü.
73.	The rice is *all* eaten . .	*Ōtsī tsō*kān*tōkā.*

74. The dhân is *all* gone . .	*Ōtscōk* ezizo kān*chākā*.
75. Put *all* the fowls together. .	*Hōnō* ōtempāŋ *nzo vātā*.
76. Put *all* the books together .	*Kāko* ōmpān *kōlōk chōi vātā*. *Kāko* hālāng*tō* (or) hetōpū *tscōsceni vātā*.
77. *All* vegetables are good .	*Hāŋ* lāntero *mhōnā*.
78. Pull *all* together . .	Hālāngtō *nzō etchiā*.
79. *All* (the whole) the village chased the tiger.	*Ōyān* ekāni *mhurr pāncho*.
80. I kept working *all* (the entire) day.	*Ānā* eng chhum *nsūndrā vāncho*.
81. Rub this *all* over . .	*Shi* hetōpūnā *mhetā*.
82. He is *almost* dead . .	*Hicho tchyūv* sālā.
83. I *almost* caught him . .	*Ānā* etsukārōnākā *shi rumhau* te.
84. He lives *alone* . . .	*Shi* nchyūāti *vānālā*. *Shi* ōmōti *vānālā*.
85 I went *alone* . . .	*Ā* mōti *wōcho*.
86. Come *along* with me . .	*Ā* pānā *rōā*.
87. He is running *along* the bank of the river.	*Pōfū rāni esānā iyālā*.
88. He has twenty cattle, I *also* have a few (several).	*Skinā māngsü mekwü li*, *ānā* hā *terāro liā*.
89. Did you tell me that Nymtsemo had *already* come?	*Nymtsemō* nthāngā *yitākātō ninā ā zōchōke?*
90. The mail-carriers go over to Themokudima *alternately*.	*Kākoā Chemangi* nnītā *thrōwālā*.
91. Come *alternate* days (every other day).	Engā vānsi, engā rōā. Engā vānsi engā rōā.
92. *Although* I am hungry I'll go	*Ā wōntōntsüng*lehā *ānā wō*.
93. *Although* I have been called I won't go.	*Ā tsātāk*lehā *m'mō*.
94. He is *altogether* bad . .	*Shicho* echūngānā *m-mhō*.
95. I will *always* stay here .	*Ānā* nchōkāpen *hello vām*.
96. Why are you *always* late? .	*No ntsōle* nchōkāpeŋ *nshichōlā?*
97. Our spirits live *always* (for ever).	*Ete lamm* nchünkō *vānālā*.
98. *Among* many houses this is the largest.	*Oki e lumm* nūngo *shi tsapōwō*.
99. This is a very *ancient* writing	*Shi erāncho e lamm* eketākā.
100. Look at the sun, moon *and* stars.	*Eng nā chōro* nā *shāntiwō zetā*.

101. Come *and* eat . . .	*Ōrō tsōā.*
102. *Another* man did it . .	Ōyāmnā *shi lyūicho.*
103. Give me *another* . .	Tāmpō *ā pīa.*
104. Put it in *another* place .	*Shi metā* pōe *vāta.*
105. Come *another* (some other) time.	Thāmōthang *rōā.*
106. If you know, why don't you *answer.*	*No nstinā, ntsōle* n'yīchōālā ?
107. There is not *any* (no) reason	Ṇtīha mak.
108. Has *any one* come ? . .	Ōchīha *rōcḥōlā ?*
109. I don't find *anybody* . .	*Anā* ōchihā *m-mḥung.*
110. I did not say *anything* to him	*Anā chi thangi* ntīhā *n-phyō.*
111. We live *apart* . . .	*Ete* champō champō *vānālā.*
112. Keep the ducks and hens *apart.*	*Hōnōnā pōtak tō* champō champō *vāntōkā.*
113. Take this *apart* (to pieces) .	*Shi* ekīlānā
114. How many *apartments* in a Naga house ?	*Kiōṉ ōkilo* nchen *kōtālā ?*
115. I gave the boys an orange *apiece.*	*Nungōr* khō *ānā khōngke picho.*
116. The Sahab gave us boys a pice *apiece.*	*Etsīnā nungōri e āko pōisā matsang tsangnā e picho.*
117. As he is *apt* to break dishes, don't put anything in his hand.	*Ōpfū kherūp keyo* tsōlānhā, *shi khelō n-tihā ti teyā.*
118. I am *apt* to break dishes .	*Āio ōpfhū kherup* tsōlān.
119. *Are* you well ? . . .	*Nō mhōmhōnā* vānālā ?
120. Who *are* you ? . . .	*Nnō ōchō* lā ?
121. They *are* here . . .	*Shiang hello* līā.
122. *As* I was going over to Kohima I met the Bor Sahib.	*Ānā Kōhīme* wō thang *etsi tsapō ntōkcho.*
123. I will do *as much as* I can, and do it well.	*Ānā* kōtātā *mhōnā nsāndranā* chītātā *ānā nsūndryū.*
124. He does *as* I tell him to do .	*Ānā* kōtō *pangnōānā* chitō *shina nsūndrīālā.*
125. He has gone *as* he said he would.	*Mpōnā yiu* tō *phyōsi* chītō *yikānā.*
126. He looks *as if* he were ill .	*Shi nōchōneri* escā *mhungātā.*
127. Do *as* I do	*Ānā* kōtō *lyūānā* chitō *lyūā.*
128. *As* you wish . . .	Nī lāmm kānyū.

129.	*As* I do not know whether your conduct is good or bad, I can't keep you.	*Ni etsōphyō mhōn chōālo m'mhō chōsānā n'tsi*-kamā *ni n'vān-tōkū.*
130.	*As* you are ill I'll go . .	*Nī rātā*kamā *ānā wō.*
131.	He went *as* far *as* the door and stopped.	*Shi kipang* nthangō *wōsi vāncho.*
132.	I'll go and *ask* what is best .	*Ntiō ntiō mhōnānā ānā* ezōlo *wō.*
133.	He is *asleep*, do not awaken him. He has awaked.	*Shi* yipāvānkā *ti n-tichhiā. Shi yipchangchitākā.*
134.	My foot is *asleep* . .	*Ā cho* zzüzzā.
135.	On hearing these words they will be much *astonished.*	*Ōyi shī zōnā shiangnā elamm* emhōkū.
136.	There is a beggar *at* the door	Kīpang *chhōntsōnchōyi nchyūhā vānā.*
137.	Look *at* me . . .	*Ā zetā.*
138.	I came to look *at* the road .	*Ānā ōlān zelo rōcho.*
139.	He is staying *at* the Sahib's house.	*Shī etsī kī vānālā.*
140.	Throw this *at* the cow . .	*Shī māngsū ephiāvā.*
141.	He is sitting *at the foot of* the tree	*Shicho ōtōng* kappi *kōkten vānā-lā.*
142.	I can't do this work *at all* .	*Ānā shi nsündryucho n-sündri-kōk.*
143.	I cannot see *at all* . .	*Ānā mhūng* n-drang.
144.	You have come *at last* .	*Nō* süllāmī *yicho.*
145.	They rose *at once* . .	*Shiangnā* ramtō *pānticho.*
146.	Go *at once* . . .	Ndrā *wōā.*
147.	He died *last autumn* . .	Lungkhamō tsungkīngo *etchhi-cho.*
148	I did not *awake* once . .	*Echūngwātīhā ānā n-*yipchang-cho.
149.	Take this *away* . . .	*Shi hānsi wōā.*
150.	It is good for nothing, throw it *away.*	*Shi ntihā m-mhō,* siā (*or*) shūmte siā.
151.	He has turned *back* . .	*Shicho* elānai *iyātākā.*
152.	The boys are all coming *back*	*Nūngōr hetōpūnā* clānai *iyālā.*
153.	He is lying on his *back* .	*Shicho* ntīkāro *yipālā.*
154.	My *back* aches . . .	*A* mānkū *ā nōālā.*
155.	I sleep at the *back side* .	*Ānā* ōchūwe *yippālā.*
156.	Come to the *back side* of the house.	*Ōki* khāntsangwe *rōā.*

157. He is walking *backwards* .	*Shīnā* scūlānphīwō *esetātsālā.*
158. He is writing *backwards* .	*Shīnā* sīlyūwō *erānālā.*
159. Why do you cut wood with such *a bad* dao.	*Nō ntōtsōle lepōk* m-mhōm *chītyunā ōtscung wōālā ?*
160. He wishes *to be* a head man of the village.	*Sīhnā gāuṇbūrā* tsōkīlàtto *tsōālā.*
161. I came *because* I wanted to .	*Erō hngcho rōcho.*
162. I went *because* you sent me .	*Nnā wōtō ā lungōchi ānā wōcho.*
163. He came *before* sunrise .	*Eng* n-chōrōthang *shīnā rōcho.*
164. I came *before* eating my rice	*Ā tsī* ṇ-tsōthung *ānā rōcho.*
165. Don't stand *before* (in front of) me.	*Ā* mhātūngī *tī chūngwōā.*
166. Where have you *been ?* .	*Nō kūwe* wōchōlā ?
167. My father has *become* blind .	*Ā pō ōmhyek* chōtākā.
168. He came *before* me . .	*Shi ą* vungī *rōcho.*
169. I 'll *begin* to read the book to-morrow.	*Ōchyuācho ānā kāko shi kāukilàtō* tscō.
170. His *behaviour* is very bad .	*Shi* etsōphiyō *tungtō m-mhō.*
171. There is a tiger *behind* that mountain.	*Pūnglān chi* engammī *mhurr vāṇ.*
172. Put my shoes *behind* the box	*Ōchen* nhkenī *ā chōkab vātā.*
173. Calves follow close *behind* their mothers.	*Māngsū ōrō chīnā ōpvū* ōscūlo *erikātā pānālā.*
174. You are *behind time.* . .	*Nīnā* n-shīthangā.
175. I don't *believe* you. . .	*Ānā ni yi* n-nūngtsū.
176. This spear *belongs* to me .	*Shicho ā tscō.*
177. Yikum village is *below* Wokha	*Yikumcho Wōkhai yān* kappī.
178. Bring the chair that is *beside* the table.	*Kōktepeṇ pīlang* nthangī *elīwōchī hāṇsī iyā.*
179. It is lost *beside* the road .	*Lāntsai* elūngte *mōni siā.*
180. There are five or six persons here *besides* me.	*Ānā hā* kātōlā *chihā tāmpō nchyu mungō tirōk vāyelā.*
181. I have another *besides* this .	*Shihā* kātōlā *enungāhā liēto.*
182. Have you another cloth *besides* this ?	*Nī scū shi* tiālo *ennūāhā lililyelā ?*
183. Which is the *best* road to Morakcho ?	*Morākchōe ewō lān kūwe* mhōmō*lā* ?
184. Among these give me the one which is *best.*	*Shiang ōnūngī kūwe* mhōms*ānā ā piā.*
185. His house is *better* than mine	*Ā kicho shi ki* mhōmō.
186. Are you *better* to-day? .	*Nchingo ni* mīmīlā ?
187. I am a little *better* . .	*Āio etchukāro* pōā.

188. Write it a little *better* than that	*Chilōnā etchukāro* mhōnkātā *erānā.*
189. Don't stand *between* us .	*E* nūngi *ti vānā.*
190. The river flows *between* the mountains.	*Pōfūcho pūnglān* yītālōnā *iyālā.*
191. I gave *between* four and five hundred rupees.	*Anā rāmpiāk nzō mezu mūngālo* nsāsā *picho.*
192. This is very *bitter* . .	*Shicho elam* khōā.
193. Bring my *black* hat . .	*Ā khikho* enyikkōchī *hānai iyā.*
194. The Sahab *blames* me . .	*Etsīnā ā* phyōphī kātālā.
195. I am not to *blame* . .	*Ā* phyōphī *n-ni.*
196. *Blow* the fire . . .	*Ōmi* mhūā.
197. The wind is *blowing* . .	*Mpōng* vênālā.
198. Has the water *boiled?* .	*Otchhü* lālāhānlā ?
199. It has not *boiled* . . .	N-lākhā.
200. It has *boiled* . . .	Elāktākā.
201. Bring *boiling* water . .	Chhīllūm *hānsī iyā.*
202. My first-*born* and also my last-*born* are here	*Ā* pōktemōchī *hā ōkāuwōchi hā hello vān.*
203. *Borrow* two rupees of the shopman.	*Nnō shīshōe thungi rāmpiāk enni* nōā.
204. Loosen *both* the ponies .	*Kōrr* ōniātā *vāchiā.*
205. Clean the *bottom* of this .	*Shi* ndre*chi scā.*
206. The *bottom* of the mountain .	*Phūnglan* chente.
207. *Break* this thread . .	*Ōying shi* chākkā.
208. Don't *break* my walking-stick	*Ā chārong ti* erānsōā.
209. *Break* this stone . . .	*Ōlung shi* phūngsōā.
210. The mat is *broken* . .	*Ōphak chi* phīchecho.
211. The stick is *broken* . .	*Otscang chi* kōchākā.
212. My leg is *broken* . .	*Ā chōke* khūchākā.
213. My tooth is *broken* . .	*Ā hō* vākūicho.
214. This mat is very long and *broad.*	*Ōphuk shī elamm suppōā elamm* nzōā.
215. We are *brothers.* . .	Enchennī.
216. They are *brothers* . .	*Shiang* ōnchennī *liā.*
217. My older *brother* and your younger *brother* are of equal height.	*Ā* tātō *nā ni* nyūīto *ōni kitī.*
218. We will go *but* you must stay	*Enī wō* sī *nnō ni vāntōkū.*
219. I hear your words, *but* I don't understand what you say.	*Ānā ni yi zōālā* tōsī *nnā utiwō phyōāsānā ānā n-tsi.*
220. *Buy* cloth	*Ōscū* shīā.

221. He is sitting *by* the door	*Shinā kipungō kōktevānālā.*
222. Stand *by* me	*Ā* escuppō *vānā.*
223. Shall we go *by* boat or afoot?	*Enī ōhrōnginā yiwālo tchhūtscainā yiūlā.*
224. I killed him *by means of* a stone.	*Ānā ōlūngnā shi ephiātsungcho.*
225. He stood *by* (up for) me	*Shinā ā yilo techo.*
226. I will come *by and by*	*Ānā* ōkhānātī *rō.*
227. Go and *call* the hogs	*Wōkō* tsālō *wōā.*
228. What is it *called?*	*Shi kūtō* (or) *ntiō* tsālā.
229. *Can* you say so or not?	*Hetyūli phyōphyō* cheūlā?
230. I *cannot* go without my cane	*Chārong n-sūnā ānā n-wō*kōk.
231. He says he *can* come tomorrow.	*Ōchō rō* cheiū *tō phyōā.*
232. I don't *care*	*Henhen tchumchākā ā tānā te kānyū.*
233. Take good *care* of everything	*Lumātungtāro tānungā zetā vānā.*
234. Go *carefully*	Tsungtsāro *wōā.*
235. Don't do your work *carelessly*	*Tī* tscōlāp phīlapnā *nsundrā.*
236. *Catch* him	*Shī* ramhā.
237. I can't *catch up* with him	*Ānā shi n*-paiyātālā.
238. I *caught* the small-pox from Nymtsemo.	*Nymtsemōnā pencho ā* kācho.
239. *Cause* this to be brought	*Shī hānsī yi*tōkā.
240. The rain has *ceased*	*Erū* pōchhītākā.
241. *Cease* the noise (don't make a noise)	*Tī nyāngnyāngā* (or) *tī pōrāktānā, siā.*
242. That bird sings *ceaselessly*	*Wōro chinā khū*pvū vānālā.
243. I will *certainly* go	*Ānā* ōtscōtscō *wō.*
244. Can you give me *change* for a rupee, or not?	Orāng tsāro *e pipikōkūlā?*
245. He has *changed* his cloth	*Shinā ōscū* thōngphīcho.
246. It is a little *chilly*	*Echakāro ezu myimālā.*
247. Take your *choice*	*Kūwe nī lummsānā ethungī khia.*
248. I *choose* this	*Shī ā* lummālā.
249. Draw a *circle*	Nkōnā *erānā.*
250. He goes around in a *circle*	*Shinā* nkōnā *hārīphiālā.*
251. This dish is *clean*	*Ōpfhu shī* ntsungdrungā.
252. *Clean* this dish	*Ōpfhu shī* scā.
253. *Clean* the path nicely	*Ōlān mhōnā* khechetā.

254. *Clear* the jungle . . .	*Ōrai chī* tsōnī sīą.
255. *Clear* out	Tsānā, tsānā, (*or*) wōā, wōā.
256. This water is *clear* . .	*Otchhü shī* ntsungā.
257. *Clear* the way (get out of the way).	*Ānkā* chīā.
258. *Close* the door . . .	*Hānkhā* khāṉnā.
259. This flower *closes up* at night	*Therā shī zamōtung* zaptālā.
260. *Close* your mouth . .	*Nipang* ntsappā.
261. *Close* your eyes . . .	*Nī ōmhyek* chōkkā.
262. Stand *close* to me . .	*Ā* nthangō nthōngā *vānā.* *Ā* escappō *vānā.*
263. It is very *cloudy* to-day .	*Nchingō mpemō elōk liā.*
264. He *clubbed* the Naga . .	*Shinā khyōṉ* lungtsuncho.
265. It is *cold* to-day . . .	*Nchingo* etsukkā.
266. The air is *cold* . . .	*Mpōng* myīmmā.
267. Bring *cold* water . .	*Otchhü* nkōng, (or) *Tchhünkōng, hānsī iyā*, (or) *Tchhü*myim *hānsī iyā.*
268. *Come* here	*Hêipi* rōā.
269. I did not *come* . . .	*Ānā n*-yīhā (*or*) *n*-yīcho. *Ānā n*-drōhā, (*or*) *n*-drōcho. *Ānā n*-tsācho.
270. I will *commence* the work now	*Nthāngā ānā nsundryūkilàttō* sākau.
271. Let us go down to the bazaar. *Come, come.*	*Bōzāre chōwātaukā vvā.* Rōālō, rōālō.
272. They came to make a *complaint* against me.	*Shiangnā ā echākechī yī erryūkilāttō rōcho.*
273. Cloth on being put in water *contracts.*	*Ōscü ōtchhülo thenā* enyethryūālā.
274. Everything is in *confusion* .	*Hetōpū* phīrōe *liā.*
275. I have no *confidence* in what he says.	*Shinā ntiō ntiwō phyōsānā ānā n*-nungtsū.
276. There is *always* (or) *constantly* a great noise here.	*Hello* nchūnkōṉ *elamm wōnyāng yī nyāngālā.*
277. The dog barks *constantly* .	*Phūrro chinā thryū*pvu vānālā.
278. He acts *contrary* to my commands.	*Ānā ntiō phyōnāchī shinā n-zō kiālā.*
279. They *could* not catch the hen	*Shiangnā hōnō n-ramhā*kōk.

General Conversation.

1. Who are you?	Sing.	*Nnō ōchiwêlā?*
	„	*Nnā ōchīlā?*

	English	Lhota
1.	Who are you?	*Nino ōchaiēla?*
	Pl. ,,	*Ntenā ōchaiēla?*
2.	I am the dâk-walla . .	*Aio kāko ehāṉ.*
3.	What village do you belong to?	*Nīnō nyū yaṉlā?*
4.	I am of Wokha . .	*Aiyo Wōkekā.*
5.	Where are you going?	*Nnō kūi wōlā?*
6.	I am going in to Themokudima.	*Ánā Chemangi threiyālā.*
7.	Whence have you come?	*Kūina ichōlā?*
8.	Day before yesterday I came up from Yikam, but to-day I came in from Wokha.	*Ōrāncho ānā Yikammenā chūngicho ōsü nchingo Wōkenā threyicho.*
9.	When will you go back again?	*Ennōāhā kōthāng wōlāmlā?*
10.	I'll go back to Wokha alone to-morrow, and after four or five days will go down to Golaghat.	*Ōchö āmoti Woke wōlām, ōsü nchōk mezü mūngō vāsü Kūlai chōwō.*
11.	Why are you going down to Golaghat?	*Ntsōle Kūlai chōwōla?*
12.	I am going down to trade, if you please.	*Shishōā chōwō kānyū.*
13.	What are you going to buy?	*Ntiō shiūla?*
14.	I am going to buy this and that, if you please.	*Lamāthangtero shilo chōwō kānyū.*
15.	Will you sell me those eggs?	*Nnō hōno chī ā shishütōkūlā?*
16.	I will not sell . . .	*N-yeṉ.*
17.	How many houses in your village?	*Ni yāncho ōki kōtāla?*
18.	One hundred and fifty or more, perhaps.	*Nzōā sü ōki thamdro ādrā kanyū.*
19.	Is there much sickness in your village or not?	*Ni yāmo phirapmōrōm elam lililā?*
20.	Not much this year, but there was much last year.	*Nnchikam phirap mōrom elam n-nī, ōsü nankamōcho phirap mōrom elam liā.*
21.	When you are sick, what do you do?	*Phiraptātāthangcho nyūwō lyūelā?*
22.	We call the medicine-man, and if we don't get well, we sacrifice.	*Enā rātsen tsāle m-pōkāmā emūlyūā.*
23.	Were your crops better this year than last year?	*Nchikam ni li mhōmōālo nankamo mhōmōlā?*

24. They were better last year.	*Nankamo mhōmo.*
25. What is the price of dhān a maund?	*Sirrü zirocho kūtā mān lā?*
26. From Rs. 1-8 to Rs. 2.	*Piākā sü poko mān ōpiāk enni mān tsō.*
27. What are you doing now-a-days on your cultivations?	*Epaiyāhicho ōlichō ntio lyūtālā?*
28. We are harvesting Konī dhān now, afterwards we will cut the Sālī dhān.	*Nthānācho enā ōten ntsānālā hesicho mātso rū.*
29. How many times do you eat in a day?	*Engiālo cho kōtā tsōālā?*
30. We eat in the morning, at noon, and in the evening, three times a day.	*Enā engiyāthang chōā tsō, n-shüethango chōā tsō, milān chōā tsō, tō engiānāchō etham tham tsōālā.*
31. Who cooks the rice? . .	*Ōchinā ōtsi rüālā?*
32. The one who stays at home cooks it.	*Kilo mūngnā rüālā.*
33. Have you a wife and children?	*Ni kikham lililā, ōtsōe lililā?*
34. I have two wives and five children.	*A khikham nchü enni ōtsoe o mūngo.*
35. Is the first-born a boy or a girl?	*Pōktemmōchü epüālō elüēlā?*
36. The first-born is a boy, ten years old.	*Pōktemmōchü epuēkamā nzü tōkūo.*
37. Do your women do coolie-work?	*Ni khikamcho kūli "kām" n-sündralā nung?*
38. They do not . . .	*Shiano n-sündrü.*
39. Get out of the way, I am going to break the rock with gunpowder.	*Ānā kōrr ke ōnūng pōkōkā, ānkā chiā, ānkā chiā.*
40. Now come and go to work .	*Nthāngā ōyi nsündrā.*
41. Send two men to bring bamboos.	*Nchü eni vepfu hānsi yitōkā.*
42. Let them rest a litte . .	*Terrāro esāntōkā.*
43. How much pay do you want a day?	*Engi engina ōtsen kōtā hngālā?*
44. I want four annas and my boy two.	*Aiyo moiyā enni ōsü ā nūngōr-cho moiyā matsangā.*
45. I can't give so small a boy so much.	*Nūngōr hetūv hetātā n-pikōk.*

46. Bring some hot water, I wish to bathe.	*Chülam hapsi iyā, ānā tsākaukiàtto tscōākā.*
47. Send them away, I'll pay them tomorrow.	*Yitōkā, ānā ōchōchi ōtsen piukā.*
48. Go to your village and get ten coolies.	*Niyāni yisü kūli nchü tāro sōsi rōā.*
49. Now you may go to get the wormwood.	*Nthāngā mhātso hāno wōtōkā.*

ENGLISH-LHOTA VOCABULARY.

ENGLISH-LHOTA VOCABULARY.

A

A (*lit.*—one) . . . *Nchūhā, matsangā, ntsangā.*
Abandon . . . *Süsi iyālā.*
Abate (as a storm) . . *Pōchaiyālā.*
Abate (as disease) . . *Enyipālā.*
Abdomen . . . *Ōso, mmā, ōpōk.*
Abduct . . . . *Mpōā sōā vānālā.*
Abet . . . . *Themō thetālā.*
Abettor . . . *Ōthemwe ethewōchü.*
Lit.—The one on his side.
Abhorrent . . . *Nkōngā, etsākā.*
Able (to be) . . . *Che* "or" *kōk* (affixed to verb).
Abide . . . . *Vānālā.*
Abode . . . . *Evān̠.*
Abortion . . . *Ngāro etchü, ngāro enūngā.*
About (nearly) . . *Hākōno, ekōno.*
About (on the point of) . *Sālā.*
Above . . . . *Mhai, ōpōni, ōyāki.*
Abreast, *adv.* . . . *Reni.*
Abreast, to stand . . *Renālā, renivānālā.*
Abscond . . . *Mpōā tsānālā.*
Absent . . . . *N-vān̠, m-mā.*
Abundance . . . *Kōshā, elam.*
Abuse, *v.* . . . *Mākālā, khōnālā.*
Accept . . . . *Khiālā.*
Accidentally . . . *N-tsühā.*
Lit.—unknowingly.
Accidentally . . . *M-mhūngā.*
Lit.—not seeing.
Accompany . . . *Pānā, nzō, sirrā, essüdrā* (with verbs signifying to come and to go.)
Accumulate . . . *Tsōtsi vātālā, shishōe vātālā.*
Accurate . . . *Ōtscōtscō, khyangā* (as a balance).
Accurate . . . *Ephen̠, khiti.*
Accuse . . . . *Phyō phiālā.*
Ache . . . . *Enōā, nōkhangā.*
Acid . . . *Thenā, thempvūrāngkātā.*

Acquaintance . . .	*Hngtāphen, ntsütāphen.*
Acquire . . .	*Piālā.*
Across . . .	*Mphiwō.*
Across . . .	*Pānkauwe.*
	Lit.—other side of.
Across, to place . .	*Rōkai vātālā.*
Act . . .	*Lyūālā.*
Acute (of pain, joy, &c.) .	*Tangto.*
Adams-apple . . .	*Ekhi.*
Add . . .	*Tsōtsi vātālā.*
Admit . . .	*Tāchūngi threyitōkā.*
Adult . . .	*Rānchākchākā.*
Adulterer . . .	*Lōmō esi, lōngsulōngphūe.*
Adultery, to commit .	*Lōmō siālā.*
Advance . . .	*Ōvangwe wōā, ōvangwe iyā.*
Advice . . .	*Ōkiāk.*
Advise . . .	*Ōkiāk piālā.*
Afar . . .	*Ekōni.*
Affectionate . . .	*Lampamchiā, lamm mhōnā.*
Afoot . . .	*Ōchōenā.*
Afraid . . .	*Khyūthātā, ekhūtsangā.*
After . . .	*Silāmwe, esilo.*
After-birth . . .	*Ōshang.*
Afternoon . . .	*Nshüchāchōlo.*
Afterwards . . .	*Ōkhānāti, ōkaicho, ōkaiti, hisi, ōkeleti* (long time).
Again . . .	*Nthāngo, eniwōhā.*
Again . . .	*Lām* "or" *lān* (affixed to verb).
Against . . .	*Engōke.*
Age . . .	*Pōksi nsu.*
	Lit.—Years after birth.
Age . . .	*Nsu kōtā?*
	Lit.—Years, how many?
Aged . . .	*Sōntsangā, sōntākā.*
Ago, (long since) . .	*Nkōlō, nkōlō ōmān tsōnā.*
Agony . . .	*Ngkak.*
Aground . . .	*Chūngthetā.*
Ague . . .	*Liōrā, yiōrā.*
Ahead . . .	*Ōvangi, mhātūngi.*
Aid . . .	*Kyōālā.*
Aim . . .	*Echūālā.*
Air . . .	*Ezzü.*

English	Lhota
Alarm	*Ekhentŏkălă.*
Alas	*Hai yo o, hă-ā, ăpāpă.*
Alien	*Ōyăm, yămpŏe.* *Lit.*—Other village.
Alike	*Khīti, myăntaktakā* (even).
Alive	*Ekam.*
All	*Ōmpă, hălăngto, hetŏpŭ, hetŏpvŭ, lănga,* and affix *tzŭ.*
Almighty	*N-sŭndrŭkŏk ntyŭhā n-ni, n-lyŭkŏk nyŭhă n-ni.* *Lit.*—Not able to do, there is nothing.
Almost	*Echŭkāro* (with a negative), *sălă.* *Lit.*—About, on the point of.
Alms	*Ōthăn.*
Alone	*Ōmōtī, ŏpōti, nchyŭăti.*
Along	*Pānă, thŏngpănā.*
Aloof	*Elŏnchŏe.*
Aloud	*Ekyŏ.*
Already	*Nthāngā.*
Also	*Hā.*
Altar	*Emŭ vāmphen, Sūtsangdhrān vamphen.*
Alter	*Ōmōchŭng lyŭālā.*
Alternately	*Nnītā, chungtā.*
Although	*Hā, āhā, tŏlehā, tŏāhā* (affixes).
Altogether	*Chōālyi.*
Altogether (wholly)	*Mpemō.*
Always	*N-chūnkō, echōng, ntchuthangŏ.*
Amazed	*Emhōktsangā.*
Ambush, to lie in	*Rāvānī vānālā.*
Amid	*Ōnŭngo.*
Among	*Ōnūngo.*
Amount	*Ōmpă.*
Ancestors	*Pyamtsa matsī.*
Ancient	*Nkōlō, ehen, ekenchākă.*
And	*Nā, sŭ, hă.*
Angami	*Tsangŏ.*
Angel	*Patsŏwo lāmphen.*
Anger	*Lamm tsōkā.*
Angle	*Nken.*
Angry	*Lamm tsōkā.*
Animal (domestic)	*Ekamtsakīlo.*

Animal (wild) . . . *Ōsōngo.*
Ankle . . . *Chōmhyek.*
Anna (4 pice) . . *Poisā mezü, rāngmyo mezü.*
Annoyance . . . *Ekhetsā.*
Annual . . . *Nzü nzü.*
Anoint . . . *Nzālā.*
Another (of things) . . *Thāmphō, pōe.*
Another (of persons) . *Ōyâm.*
Answer . . . *Yīchōālā.*
Ant (black) . . . *Tscamphiro enyiko.*
Ant (red) . . . *Tscamphiro emyōmō.*
Ant (white) . . . *Tscamphiro mmiwō.*
Ant (winged) . . . *Tscamphiro tsiphiā.*
Ant-hill . . . *Tscamphiro yōcho.*
Ant-nest . . . *Tscamphiro shab.*
Antler . . . *Sepvū echū.*
Anxious . . . *Ekhentsangā.*
Anybody . . . *Ōchiā, ōyān̲.*
Anything . . . *Nyūhā, n-tīhā.*
Anywhere . . . *Kūhā, kūlōhā.*
Apart . . . *Chūngchūngnā, champō champō.*
Apart (take), *v.* . . *Ekilānālā.*
Apartment . . . *Nchen̲.*
Ape . . . *Ōtam.*
Apiece . . . *Matsang tsango.*
Appear . . . *Chiālā.*
Appearance . . . *Ōphyō.*
Appetite . . . *Wōntōntsangā.*
Applaud . . . *Tsaiyālā.*
Approve . . . *Mhōnā zechetā.*
Approach . . . *Escappō rōālā, nthangō rōālā.*
Approach . . . *Escappō wōālā.*
Archer . . . *Ōlō ephen̲.*
Arise . . . *Pānthiālā.*
Arm (of body) . . *Ewōn̲.*
Armlet . . . *Kōrro.*
Armour . . . *Phīpō sampō.*
Around . . . *Hrīpiā, nkōn̲.*
Arouse . . . *Ntechiā.*
Arrest . . . *Ōlān̲ khānyālā, ntālānchiālā.*
Arrive . . . *Chānālā.*
Arrow . . . *Lōtsü.*
Artery . . . *Chempvu.*

Article . . . *Thārāpvūro, khikyōnikyō.*
As much as . . . *Kōtā tātā.*
As, so . . . *Kōtō chitō.*
Ascent . . . *Chūngwālā.*
Ashamed . . . *Yikrālā.*
Ashes . . . *Mīpōk.*
Aside . . . *Epōmwe.*
Aside (stand) . . . *Enkāchiā.*
Aside (set) . . . *Vai yālā.*
Ask . . . *Engālā.*
Aslant . . . *Yōphiā.*
As much, so much . . *Kōtā hetātā, kōtāsānā tātā.*
Assemble . . . *Sānthryuālā.*
Assembled . . . *Etsü thryūchākā.*
Assembly . . . *Kyōn etsū thri.*
Assist . . . *Kyōālā.*
Asleep . . . *Yipthechākā.*
Associate . . . *Nzōevān, echauro, nzōeke.*
Astonish . . . *Emhōktsangā.*
At once . . . *Nthāngā, ndrā.*
Attention, to give . . *Engālā.*
Auction . . . *Ōyi tsōtā.*
Aunt (paternal) . . *Ōnō.*
Aunt (maternal) . . *Ōpvurām.*
Auspices . . . *Tsenphikhangā.*
Await . . . *Zetā vānā.*
Awake . . . *Yipyangchiālā.*
Awaken . . . *Nthechiālā.*
Awe . . . *Lamm thōtōkā.*
Axe . . . *Opvhū.*

B

Babe . . . *Ngāro.*
Babyhood . . . *Ngāro thang.*
Bachelor . . . *Khyang drōe.*
Back . . . *Mānkū, silāmwe.*
Back (side of house) . *Khāntsang.*
Back (side of bed) . . *Ōchūwe.*
Backdoor . . . *Khāntsang.*
Backwards . . . *Silāmphiwō.*
" Backsheesh " . . *Ōthān.*
Bacon . . . *Sōnkōng, sōhen.*

Bad . . .	*M-mho.*
Bad . . .	*Verōkā.*
Bad . . .	*Hārōkhangā.*
Bag . . .	*Ozü scü.*
Bag (money) . . .	*Rāngscūkhū.*
Baggage . . .	*Khīkhyo nyikyō.*
Bait (for fish) . . .	*Ōrā.*
Balance . . .	*Efhū.*
Bald . . .	*Ōtōn phyāngā.*
Bale . . .	*Otchhü wōchōkchīālā.*
Ball . . .	*Ekā.*
Bamboo . . .	*Nkyep, vepfū, puhrü.*
Band (of music) . .	*Phīyūyūckhūe.*
Band (waist) . . .	*Rōkab.*
Bank (of river) . .	*Tchhütsen̲.*
Banner . . .	*Sīmyō.*
Banquet . . .	*Ōsho.*
Barber . . .	*Kurretsen̲.*
Bare . . .	*Khūso mpen̲scü n-khī.*
Barefaced . . .	*N-yikrā.*
Bark, *v.* . . .	*Thryūālā.*
Bark, *n.* . . .	*Tsangfū.*
Barn . . .	*Ōsōn.*
Barrel (of a gun) . .	*Tsangepvu.*
Barren . . .	*Mpōkōk, nthīkōk.*
Barter . . .	*Thōngtālā.*
Base . . .	*Chamchākā.*
Bashful . . .	*Eyikrāthātā.*
Basin . . .	*Ōpfhū.*
Bask . . .	*Engī ekhangālā.*
Basket . . .	*Ōkhyāk.*
Basket (of open work) .	*Ōkhyū.*
Basket (for carrying water)	*Khangdro.*
Bastard . . .	*Mōtso.*
Bat . . .	*Sōsīro.*
Bathe . . .	*Tsakātālā.*
Batten . . .	*Tsītam.*
Battle . . .	*Ōrrü nangthātā.*
Bawl . . .	*Khyau khangā.*
Bazar . . .	*Shīshōphen̲.*
Bead . . .	*Yōko.*
Beak . . .	*Emen̲.*

Beam . . . *Khyūro.*
Bean . . . *Ōhro.*
Bear (a burden) . . *Hānāla.*
Bear (fruit) . . . *Ekhīālā.*
Bear, *n.* . . . *Sevā.*
Beard . . . *Khokahm, koshipvā.*
Beast (wild) . . . *Romhōnī ōsōngo.*
Beast (tame) . . . *Ekam tsōkilo, ekam sōngo.*
Beat . . . *Tāpālā, taptālā, sātālā.*
Beat (a drum) . . . *Tamphiālā.*
Beautiful . . . *Zenā tangto mhōnā, eze mhōm phirōā.*
Because . . . Particle *kamā* affixed to verb.
Beckon . . . *Eyōpālā, eyimīnānthang myenala.*
Bed . . . *Yipphen.*
Bedding . . . *Saiyiphen.*
Bedrid . . . *Yipvūchiā.*
Bee . . . *Otscāk.*
Beef . . . *Māngsūso.*
Before, *adv.* (time) . . *Nthōng, ntōthang, ōvangi.*
Before, *adv.* (place) . . *Mhātūngī, ōvangwe.*
Beg . . . *Chōnchōnī tsōālā.*
Beggar . . . *Chōng kūchōntse.*
Beget . . . *Ngāro hāntōkālā.*
Begin . . . *Tscōālā,* and verbal affix *sālā.*
Begone . . . *Īyā īyā, wōā wōā.*
Behaviour . . . *Etsōphyo.*
Behead . . . *Kurr nyākīālā.*
Behind . . . *Sīlāmwe, ndrewe.*
Behold . . . *Zetā.*
Belch . . . *Nkhīchiālā.*
Believe . . . *Nangtsālā.*
Bell . . . *Ōphīang.*
Bellow . . . *Nrōngālā.*
Belly . . . *Ōpōk.*
Beloved . . . *Nzān mōchū.*
Below . . . *Ōkapi, ōkapwe, lōkokwe.*
Belt . . . *Ōscū kāphen.*
Bench . . . *Evān, khōktephen.*
Bend . . . *Kōnphiālā, nkhūthetālā.*
Benefit . . . *Nzānā.*
Beneath . . . *Ōkapī, lōkokwe.*
Benevolent . . . *Nungphiā.*

Bequeath . . . *Eyi tchhütai iyālā.*
Beside . . . *Tsātsōkwe.*
Besides . . . Affix *tiālo* followed by *chịha.*
Best . . . *Mhōmo.*
Bet . . . *Ngāngtālā, ngānsitālā, merāngtālā.*
Betel . . . *Ōshāngwō.*
Betray . . . *Ekhap kiālā.*
Betrothed . . . *Ōkīkamo, ōkikhamm.*
Betroth . . . *Sōāvānālā.*
Better . . . *Mhōmo.*
Between . . . *Yitālo, ōnūngo.*
Beyond . . . *Engamī, yākā.*
Big . . . *Tsāphō, sapo* (tall, long).
Bile . . . *Lātchicho otchhü.*
Bill (of bird) . . . *Emeṉ.*
Bind . . . *Changālā, sheṉālā, hōkālā.*
Bird . . . *Wōro.*
Bird-cage . . . *Wōro vangpheṉ.*
Bird-nest . . . *Wōro shab.*
Birth, to give . . . *Pōkālā, khīālā, ndrōālā.*
Birthplace . . . *Epōkyāṉ.*
Bisect . . . *Pōksōālā, rāsōālā.*
Bit . . . *Echükāro.*
Bitch . . . *Fhūro ōkyū.*
Bite . . . *Engkakālā.*
Bite . . . *Ōkhū.*
Bitter . . . *Khōā.*
Blabber . . . *Ōyī pōnkhaṉgā.*
Black . . . *Nyikā.*
Blacksmith . . . *Yōnchōe.*
Bladder . . . *Tchhicham.*
Blade . . . *Ōwo, yōwo, yōwe.*
Blame, *v.* . . . *Phiō kātālā, ntanālā.*
Blame, *n.* . . . *Phiōphī.*
Blank (point of a target-at which aim is taken) . *Echyū kāpheṉ.*
Blank (paper) . . . *Kāko n-rāṉcho.*
Blanket . . . *Mpempeṉ.*
Blaze . . . *Kiālā.*
Bleat . . . *Erōnālā.*
Bleed . . . *Echeṉ chīrōālā.*

Blind . . .	*Ōmhyek echang.*
Blister . . .	*Pŭchapā.*
Blockhead . . .	*Yimsirrā.*
Blood . . .	*Echeṉ.*
Bloom . . .	*Ekhisō chiālā.*
Blossom . . .	*Ekhi.*
Blow (wind) . . .	*Vĕrālā.*
Blow (breeze) . . .	*Esāpālā.*
Blow (with the mouth) .	*Mhūālā.*
Blue (indigo) . .	*Nishakūrkā.*
Blue . . .	*Myāk tsetsetā.*
Blunt . . .	*Seseto.*
Boar . . .	*Wōko ōpōng.*
Boar (wild) . . .	*Oni.*
Board . . .	*Pilang.*
Boaster . . .	*Tsōpōro tsōkhangā.*
Boat . . .	*Ōhrōng.*
Boatman . . .	*Ōhrōng ekam.*
Body . . .	*Ōtsak.*
Boil . . .	*Elākālā, shenālā, letālā, vapālā.*
Boiling water . . .	*Chhūlam.*
Bold . . .	*Lammkhangā.*
Bone . . .	*Ōrrü.*
Book . . .	*Kāko.*
Border . . .	*Scücham.*
Bore . . .	*Nyālā.*
Born . . .	*Pōkālā, ndrōālā.*
Borrow . . .	*Ōchhi epvwālā, nsōala.*
Borrowed . . .	*Nsōchākā.*
Borrow on credit . .	*Epvwi hāṉsi yichākā.*
Borrower . . .	*Ōchhü epwi, nsōe.*
Bosom . . .	*Takki.*
Both . . .	*Ōni.*
Bottle . . .	*Ewōmpvü.*
Bottom . . .	*Ndre, chōe.*
Bough . . .	*Khero.*
Boundary . . .	*Errü.*
Bow . . .	*Ōlō.*
Bow (salute) . . .	*Khamālā.*
Bowels . . .	*Mmā.*
Bow-string . . .	*Lōsü.*
Bowl . . .	*Ōpfū.*

Bow-legged . . .	*Nkōkyūā.*
Box . . .	*Ōchen.*
Boy . . .	*Nūngōrr.*
Bracelet (men) . .	*Khekhap.*
Bracelet (women) . .	*Rampam.*
Brain . . .	*Pentā.*
Branch . . .	*Khero.*
Brass . . .	*Yōnchāk.*
Brave . . .	(*See* "Bold").
Bread . . .	*Mhurr, hmdrr.*
Breadth . . .	*Nsōā.*
Break . . .	*Khūchākā.*
Break . . .	*Khirāpālā.*
Break (off a small piece) .	*Vāchōālā.*
Break (stone) . . .	*Phangsōālā.*
Break (stick) . . .	*Erānsōālā.*
Break (by the foot) . .	*Hnyechākā.*
Break (by bending over in hands).	*Erānchākālā.*
Break (by splitting lengthwise).	*Kabsōālā, phangsōālā, vasōālā.*
Breath . . .	*Ethak.*
Breathe . . .	*Ethak echenālā.*
Breeches . . .	*Chōpōkthe.*
Breeze . . .	*Ziro, esü.*
Brethren . . .	*Ōchenōnyūi*
Bribe, *v.* . . .	*Khapālā.*
Bribe, *v.* . . .	*Ekhabpiālā.*
Bribe, *n.* . . .	*Ekhav, ekhab.*
Bride . . .	*Ōki khamm.*
Bridegroom . . .	*Ōkī khammō.*
Bridge . . .	*Ōpho.*
Bridle . . .	*Korr sü.*
Bright . . .	*Tsanglāpā, tsanglelāpā.*
Brim . . .	*Pvüpang.*
Brimful . . .	*Phyangā.*
Bring . . .	*Hānai īyālā, hānsi iyālā, hānstrōālā.*
Brittle . . .	*Tsak tsakto.*
Broad . . .	*Nso.*
Broken . . .	*Khirapchākā, khūchākā.*
Brook . . .	*Tchhüso.*
Broom . . .	*Chakchā.*

Brother (younger) . .	*Ōnyüī.*
Brother (older) . .	*Ōtā.*
Brother-in-law . .	*Ōhrā.*
Brow (eye) . . .	*Mhyek kōn̲.*
Brown . . .	*Nyikshōkā.*
Bruise . . .	*Chenālā.*
Brush . . .	*Khetālā.*
Bubble . . .	*Mpen̲.*
Buck . . .	*Kātsōn̲ ōpōng, hōlyū, ōpōng.*
Bucket . . .	*Ōtchhü wōphen̲.*
Bud . . .	*Therā pvūpam.*
Buffalo . . .	*Züzü.*
Bug . . .	*Ōrrā.*
Bugle . . .	*Phiyūkhūphen̲.*
Build . . .	*Tscōālā.*
Building . . .	*Ōki.*
Bull . . .	*Māngsü ōpōng.*
Bullet . . .	*Tsangetsang.*
Bull-frog . . .	*Ōvū.*
Bullock . . .	*Māngsü nchōtsōncho.*
Bunch (of flowers) . .	*Therā vang.*
Bundle (of wood) . .	*Ōtsang pāmpōng.*
Bundle . . .	*Ōchang.*
Burden . . .	*Ōhā.*
Burn . . .	*Rōngālā, nshükātā* (scorch).
Burst . . .	*Ethang hrapā.*
Bury . . .	*Chūthetālā, shōthetālā.*
Bush . . .	*Ōzüyo.*
Business . . .	*Nsūndryū.*
But . . .	*Tōsū; ōsu.*
Butt . . .	*Shūngtālā.*
Butterfly . . .	*Süsān̲ phiyūc, sishāpilūe.*
Button . . .	*Ōscū khāphen̲.*
Buy . . .	*Shiālā.*
Buzz . . .	*Vüvālā.*
By (by means of) . .	*Nā.*
By and by . . .	*Ōkhānāti, ōkhaicho.*
By-path . . .	*Lāmpōro.*

C

Cackle (after laying) .	*Selākālā.*
Cackle (cluck) . .	*Kōkālā.*

Cactus . . . *Māngyo.*
Cage (bird) . . . *Hōno vangphen̲.*
Calendar . . . *Tsangō kaphen̲ kāko.*
Calf . . . *Māngsüro.*
Calf (of leg) . . . *Ndrān̲.*
Call . . . *Tsālā.*
Can . . . *Che, kok, hrak* (verbal affixes).
Candlestick . . . *Tangrāchōngphen̲.*
Cane (rattan) . . . *Ōrru.*
Cane (walking-stick) . *Chārōng.*
Cap . . . *Khīkho.*
Captive . . . *Evang.*
Captive (to make) . . *Vangālā.*
Capture . . . *Rhamālā.*
Carcass . . . *Etchhütsak, ōmang.*
Care for . . . *Enhyākā vānālā, zetāvānālā.*
Careful (be) . . . *Tsangtsārōā.*
Carefully . . . *Rārangā, enātō, tsangtsārō.*
Careless . . . *Tsōlap phyōlapā.*
Carry . . . *Hānālā.*
Carry (a child on the back) *Pūālā.*
Carry (a shield) . . *Ōtsōng phūālā.*
Cask . . . *Sōkō chen̲.*
Cast away . . . *Siālā, shamthesiālā.*
Castrate . . . *Nchho tshōnālā.*
Caste . . . *Ekūhrr.*
Cat . . . *Ōlyūro.*
Cat (wild) . . . *Tsaphi.*
Cataract . . . *Ngetang.*
Catch . . . *Hramātālā.*
Catch (disease) . . *Kātalā.*
Catch, up, with, overtake . *Paiyātalā, phānyātālā.*
Caterpillar . . . *Mōmō.*
Cattle . . . *Māngsü.*
Causeless . . . *Ntühā n-ni.*
Cave . . . *Mungkūo.*
Cease . . . *Ōsā.*
Cease (raining) . . *Pōtchīālā.*
Centipede . . . *Tsütsü nkaktā.*
Centre . . . *Ōnūngo.*
Certainly . . . *Ōtscōtscō.*
Chaff . . . *Mākū.*
Chair . . . *Khōktephen, evān̲.*

Chalk . . . *Ōchōṉ emhū.*
Change (exchange) . *Tōngtālā.*
Change (small money) . *Tsāro.*
Channel . . . *Zukhū.*
Charcoal . . . *Mihā.*
Chase . . . *Yūngtālā.*
Chaste . . . *Ntsōā.*
Cheap . . . *Ōmāṉlā, ōmāṉ elāro, lālōkwā.*
Cheat . . . *Etchụ phiālā.*
Checked . . . *Sesōā.*
Cheek . . . *Eyå.*
Chest . . . *Taki* (the breast).
Chest (box) . . . *Ōcheṉ.*
Chew . . . *Mechā metālā.*
Chicken . . . *Hōnoro.*
Chief . . . *Ekhang.*
Child . . . *Ōtsōe.*
Child (male) . . . *Ōtsōe epuē, āngo.*
Child (female) . . *Tsōelāngo, ōtsōe elūē rōro, ākā.*
Child (only) . . . *Epōnthi.*
Child (grand) . . . *Ōriwō.*
Child (infant) . . . *Ngāro.*
Childhood . . . *Ngāro thang.*
Chill (with fever) . . *Liōrā.*
Chilly . . . *Terā etsākā.*
Chin . . . *Khōkā, khōkāṉ.*
Chirp . . . *Erōnālā.*
Choice . . . *Lamm.*
Choke . . . *Nhyangālā.*
Cholera . . . *Phyōtātā.*
Choose . . . *Lammālā.*
Chop . . . *Tānālā.*
Cigar . . . *Mekūwō shūcho.*
Circle . . . *Nkōnā, ekā.*
Circuitous . . . *Nkoṉ, hāriphiā.*
Circular . . . *Hāriphiā, ekālālākā.*
Claw (fore), *n.* . . *Yinkep, yenkyep.*
Claw (hind) . . . *Chōyinkyep.*
Claw, *v.* . . . *Nshākālā.*
Clay . . . *Phūyūcho.*
Clean . . . *Ntsangā.*
Clean, *v.* (as dishes) . *Siālā, nsālā.*

Clean, *v.* (with brush or broom) . . . *Khetālā.*
Clear . . . *Ntsangā.*
Climb . . . *Chūngwālā.*
Cling (twine around) . *Yōkātālā.*
Cling (as plaster) . . *Tsōkātā, zāpkāta.*
Clock . . . *Ōzeṉ.*
Close (near) . . . *Nthangō, essapō, enghyānō.*
Close, *v.* (as the mouth) . *Ntsapalā.*
Close, *v.* (as the eyes) . *Chōkālā.*
Close, *v.* (as a door) . . *Khānālā.*
Close, *v.* (as a drawer) . *Techiālā.*
Close, *v.* (up, as a flower) . *Zaptālā.*
Closely (to sow) . . *Eyingā yingālā, renta yingālā.*
Cloth . . . *Ōscū.*
Cloth . . . *Silam* (with wide white stripes and narrow dark ones).
Cloth . . . *Lūngkiscū* (with wide dark stripes and narrow white ones).
Cloth . . . *Pāndrap* (dark blue).
Cloth . . . *Simyō* (red).
Clothe . . . *Mpenālā.*
Clothe (causative) . . *Mpentōkālā.*
Clothing . . . *Pipōsampō.*
Cloud . . . *Elōk.*
Club . . . *Sātāpheṉ.*
Club, *v.* . . . *Sālā.*
Cluck . . . *Kōkōkālā.*
Cluster . . . *Vang.*
Coal . . . *Mihā.*
Coal (live coal) . . *Miroṉ.*
Coarse (of cloth) . . *Peshīpeshito.*
Coat . . . *Sōkthescū.*
Cob (corn) . . . *Tsangodhrotōng.*
Cobweb . . . *Pōrāktsūtsū.*
Cock . . . *Hāmpōng.*
Cock-crow . . . *Hōno khūāthang.*
Cocoanut . . . *Hōkātōng.*
Cohabit . . . *Yūtālā, lyūtāyipālā, ntsangtālā.*
Coil . . . *Shāthrūālā, pāthrūālā.*
Cold . . . *Myimā, nkōng.*
Cold, to be . . . *Etsakālā, etsaktsangā.*

Cold season . . . *Etsako.*
Collect . . . *Khōlōktscōī vātālā, tsōtsenī vātālā.*
Collect (revenue) . . *Lōkōtsen khīālā.*
Colt . . . *Korrōro.*
Comb, *n.* . . . *Eshā, kurr khephen.*
Comb, *v.* . . . *Nshākālā, ōtscān khetālā.*
Comb (of a fowl) . . *Hōno hāntscāk, hōnōscenphiāk.*
Come . . . *Yīālā, rōālā, tsātālā.*
Coming . . . *Ōro.*
Command . . . *Pangnōālā.*
Commandment . . *Pangnōcho.*
Commerce . . . *Shītā.*
Companion . . . *Ntangō evān, essapo evān, nzō evān.*
Compel . . . *Tōkālā* (causative verbal affix).
Compassion . . . *Nzān.*
Complain . . . *Ethochakkālā.*
Complete . . . *Metākā.*
Completed . . . *Metakchākā.*
Complexion . . . Light as of Europeans—*mmiā.* Dark as of Chota Nagpore—*enyik.* Fairly light as an average Babu or Naga—*sōhākū.* A little darker than the above—*sōmyō.* A little darker still—*sōnyek.*
Comprehend . . . *Ntsiā.*
Comrade . . . *Nzō evān, nzo eke.*
Concave . . . *Ekōkā.*
Conceal . . . *Mpōe vātālā.*
Concerning . . . *Yī.*
Couch . . . *Yipen, echen, pilang.*
Conduct . . . *Etsōphyō.*
Confide . . . *Lammī ntiō nchamānāchi ezōkānālā.*
Confine . . . *Vāngālā.*
Confusion . . . *Phyensōrāvā, shamrōshamtsiā.*
Conquer, *v.* . . . *Tōā.*
Consider . . . *Echamī zetālā, nchamī zetālā.*
Constantly . . . *Pvu* (verbal affix).
Contend . . . *Pāngtālā.*
Content . . . *Lammchantangā, lammchangchāngā.*
Contain . . . *Tsōā, thetālā.*
Contemn . . . *N-zehngālā.*
Continue . . . *Vānālā.*

Continually . . .	*Nchakāpen, pvu* (verbal affix).
Converse . . .	*Chāntālā, ezōtālā.*
Convert . . .	*Thāmphō nchhamālā.*
Convey . . .	*Hānsi yiālā.*
Cook (rice and curry) .	*Otsihān nsandrālā.*
Cook (rice) . . .	*Otsi rālā.*
Cook (curry) . . .	*Ohān ekhūālā, Ōhān vapālā.*
Cook-house . . .	*Tsōyāmphenī, tsoyānkī, tsīraki.*
Cool . . .	*Echakāro nkōngā, echakāro myemā.*
Copious . . .	*Khōshā.*
Copper . . .	*Yōnchāk.*
Cord . . .	*Ōzzü, etho.*
Cork (stopper) . .	*Ndhren, nthretā.*
Corn . . .	*Tōngpālāk tsütsüng, tsangōnthro.*
Corner . . .	*Nken.*
Corpse . . .	*Ōmang.*
Correct . . .	*Ōtscōtscō.*
Cost . . .	*Ōmān, mān.*
Costly . . .	*Ōmān tsākā, ōmān elam.*
Cotton . . .	*Khōngkhō.*
Cotton tree . . .	*Khōngkhōtōng.*
Cough, *v.* . . .	*Ekhūālā, hāktsiālā.*
Cough, *n.* . . .	*Ekhūā.*
Counsel (to hold a) . .	*Sānthrīchāntālā.*
Count . . .	*Khālā.*
Countenance . . .	*Ōphyōn.*
Counterfeit (money) .	*Rāngtap, ōrāng ntapō, rāngyimō.*
Counterfeit (death) *v.* .	*Etchīra tsōālā.*
Counterfeit (sleep) *v.* .	*Yipthetālā.*
Country . . .	*Metā.*
Couple . . .	*Ōnī, ōmpōē* (male and female).
Couple . . .	*Tsōngkō* (spoken of the feet and hands).
Courageous . . .	*Ntyūhā ekū ntsü, lammkhangā.*
Court-house . . .	*Yānkī.* *Lit.*—Village house.
Cousin . . .	*Pōtsōchenī.*
Cover, *v.* . . .	*Hlāpālā, ventālā.*
Cover (the mouth with the hands).	*Emen efwiālā, emen zammiālā.*
Cover (as seed with dirt) .	*Scōzālā.*
Cover, *n.* . . .	*Hlāphen.*
Covet . . .	*Ekhīyū nchamālā.*

Cow . . . *Māngsü ōkhyū.*
Cowardly . . . *Kāphyōkā, ndre nsapkhangā.*
Cowherd . . . *Māngsü sīraphi.*
Coy . . . *Yikrātā.*
Crab . . . *Hāpūro, hāpvūro.*
Crack, *n* . . . *Ekak.*
Crack, *v* . . . *Rakālā.*
Cracked . . . *Khūngsōchākā.*
Cramp . . . *Tscāngālā.*
Crawling . . . *Epvā vānā.*
Crazy . . . *Zuvā, zuvālā.*
Cream . . . *Pōshāng, pōshāngā.*
Cream (is rising on the milk). *Shīrotzü ōmhā pōshangālā.*
Creep . . . *Epvūchetālā, yāngkātālā.*
Creeper . . . *Ōzu eyōwo.*
Creek . . . *Tchhüro.*
Crest (of bird) . . *Hāntsān̲k.*
Cricket . . . *Yoro.*
Cries . . . *Kiālā.*
Cripple . . . *Ōchō ōkhe m-mhō.*
Crooked . . . *Khānkhūā.*
Crop . . . *Ōlī.*
Crops . . . *Tsōphen̲ ephen̲.*
Cross . . . *Lamm tsokhangā.*
Cross, to look . . . *Ōmhā ekhūālā, emen̲ nkhapālā.*
Crosswise . . . *Mphiwō, evaktāvā.*
Crotch . . . *Esham.*
Crow, *n.* . . . *Kāshāk.*
Crow, *v.* . . . *Khūālā.*
Crumb, *n.* . . . *Mānīro.*
Crumble . . . *Emeruālā.*
Crush . . . *Shārūālā, khīrapālā, epāhrapālā.*
Cry . . . *Khiāpālā, khiālā.*
Cubical . . . *Kupiāk rakātā.*
Cucumber . . . *Yishākchi.*
Cuff, *v.* . . . *Tamtālā, tamālā.*
Cultivation . . . *Ōlī.*
Cup . . . *Opfū, otchhüyūphen̲.*
Cure . . . *Tānangchetā, süphichetā.*
Curl (of hair) . . . *Ōtscān̲ khānkhūā.*
Current (of a stream) . *Otchüerru.*

Curry . . . *Ōhāṉ.*
Curse, *v.* . . . *Yōsōkhānālā.*
Curse, *v.* . . . *Sukyang m-mhōm phiālā, ezaptōkālā.*
Cushion . . . *Nkhamphen̲.*
Custom . . . *Eshukū, shikū, shukū, etsōphyo.*
Cut . . . *Nangchetālā, süthechiālā.*
Cut . . . *Nangālā, tenālā.*

D

Daily . . . *Nchakāpen̲, nchakānā.*
Dainty . . . *Ōpang nkhang.*
Dam, *v.* . . . *Ōphyō zapālā.*
Dam, *n.* . . . *Ōphyō zāphen̲.*
Damaged . . . *Yūsōrāvā.*
Dance . . . *Elhālā, ekhiōlākālā, lahlātālā.*
Dark (color or complexion) *Mangthetāpā, mangthetākā.*
Dark . . . *Mangkhangā.*
Dark (to be) . . . *Mangālā.*
Darkness . . . *Mangā.*
Dash . . . *Siekhanghrāpā.*
Daughter . . . *Ōkā, lāngō.*
Daughter-in-law . . *Ōhrām.*
Dawn . . . *Engi chirōsāthang.*
Day . . . *Nchōk, tsangō, engyā.*
Daybreak . . . *Engichirōpangō.*
Day-dawn . . . *Engyāthang.*
Day-light . . . *Tāngtāngto.*
Day (next, to-morrow) . *Ōchyū, ochö.*
Day before yesterday . *Ōrāṉ.*
Day by day . . . *Nchakāpen̲, nchakānō.*
Day (to-day) . . . *Nchüng, nching.*
Days (now-a-days) . . *Tsun̲gō ākhūā, epaiyā.*
Day's journey . . *Engāetsā.*
Dazzle . . . *Erāthāta, erātsangā.*
Dead . . . *Tchhiā.*
Deaf . . . *Enōpangā.*
Dear . . . *Enzānā.*
Dear (high-priced) . . *Tsakā, tsen khekhangā.*
Death-bed . . . *Etchhipangō.*
Debt . . . *Ōchhi, ōchhü.*
Debt (to make) . . *Nōpālā.*

Debt (to pay)	*Ŏchhi lōāla.*
Debtor	*Ōchhi epvūi.*
Decay	*Kiōnālā.*
Decayed	*Kiōnchākā.*
Deceive	*Etchüpkiālā.*
Decked	*Phipōā.*
Decline	*N-khiā.*
Declivity	*Chenkhü.*
Deep	*Chūngwā.*
Deer	*Sepvū.*
Defaced	*Erā, mpā.*
Defeated	*Tsāntokchākā.* *Lit.*—Caused to flee.
Defend	*Nkōālā, pyōnālā.*
Defender	*Nkōwōchi, phyōnchōwōchi.*
Deficient	*Zāngkhangā.*
Deformed	*Emū.*
Delay	*Enhyākā.*
Delight	*Emāthōkalā.*
Delighted, to be	*Emātsangā, emāthātālā.*
Delirium	*Zavā.*
Deliver up	*Hramipiā, vāchiālā.*
Demon	*Ōmōn.*
Den	*Kū.*
Dense	*Chāmchākā, nkhangā.*
Deny	*Echang ekhiālā, ekhiālā.*
Deride	*Chālātālā, yikrātōkālā.*
Descend	*Chōwālā, choiyālā.*
Descendants	*Ōtsōereko.*
Desire	*Chōnālā, tscōālā, hngālā.*
Despise	*Engkōngā.*
Destroy	*Yōsōrālā.*
Devour	*Tsōkhānālā.*
Dew	*Yenchū, yentsōn.*
Dhan	*Ōtsōk.*
Dhan-house	*Oshōn.*
Dhoby	*Ōscüetsci.*
Diagonal (of cloth)	*Episcū.*
Diarrhœa	*Phyōtācho.*
Die	*Tchhiala.*
Different	*Thampho, chūng chūng, yipō yipō, champō champō.*

Different . . . *Pōe* (affixed to nouns).
Difficult . . . *Khangā.*
Dig . . . *Chiālā.*
Dig-out . . . *Khōchetālā.*
Diligent . . . *Kōntsangā.*
Dilute . . . *Otchhü sakiā.*
Diminish, *v. trans.* . . *Zānkātōkālā.*
Diminish, *v. intrans.* . *Zānkātālā.*
Dip . . . *Rrüthechiālā, thechiālā.*
Direction . . . *We.*
Direction, this . . *Epīwe, hepīwe.*
Direction, that . . *Ōchīwe.*
Directly (now, at once) . *Nthāngā.*
Directly (after a little) . *Esangāro vāsu.*
Dirty . . . *Myenā.*
Disappear . . . *Engamō iyālā.*
Disappear (as clouds) . *Sākchōchiālā.*
Disbelieve . . . *N-nangtsālā.*
Discharge (dismiss) . *M-māntōkālā.*
Discharge (a debt) . . *Otchü lōālā.*
Disclose . . . *Chichepiālā.*
Disease . . . *Pīrapthātā.*
Dish . . . *Ōpfhu.*
Dish (a boat-shaped dish) . *Ōkung, ōkōn.*
Dishonest . . . *Tāchō elam, ōyī n-tsā.*
Dismal (weather) . . *Tsanglā m-mho.*
Dismembered . . . *Mangtam.*
Dismiss . . . *Wōtōkālā.*
Disobey . . . *N-zō, ng-ālā.*
Disobedient . . . *Ōyī ng-ā, chānchon-zo, ezōcho n-zo.*
Displease . . . *Ezāpālā.*
Dispute . . . *Pāngtālā, ekhīrāntālā.*
Distant . . . *Ekōnī, kōnā.*
Distant (very) . . . *Elam kōnā, lānkōnā, lankōnī.*
Distinct (separate) . . *Champō champō.*
Distinctly . . . *Rārangā.*
Distress, *n.* . . . *Ezapā.*
Distress, *v.* . . . *Ezaptōkālā.*
Distribute . . . *Chitaiyālā.*
Distrust . . . *N-nangtsālā.*
Ditch . . . *Zükūro.*
Dive . . . *Chūngthetālā.*

Divide . . .	*Chütālā* (share).
Divide (halve) . . .	*Ōnūngōnā tānsōālā, ōnūngōnā pōksōālā.*
Divorce . . .	*Pyōntālā.*
Divorced . . .	*Ōyānā sicho.*
Dizzy . . .	*Ngārā.*
Do . . .	*Lūālā, lyūālā, nsündrālā.*
Doctor . . .	*Rātsen.*
Dog . . .	*Fhūrrō.*
Domestic . . .	*Ekam, chenchiengai.*
Domestic animals . .	*Ekam tsakilā.*
Door . . .	*Hānkhā.*
Door-way . . .	*Kiphen, kipang.*
Double . . .	*Chapchetā.*
Double, *v.* . . .	*Chapchetālā.*
Dove . . .	*Vefū.*
Down (birds) . .	*Mhūro.*
Downright (perpendicular).	*Ntōngkāchiā.*
Down . . .	*Chō.*
Dowry . . .	*Engoman, ōkikhamman.*
Drag (along on the ground)	*Süālā.*
Drain . . .	*Zkhüro.*
Draw (water) . . .	*Rānālā.*
Draw (a line) . .	*Setālā.*
Draw (a fire with a stick) .	*Hlapālā, hlālā.*
Dream, *n.* . . .	*Ōmang.*
Dream, *v.* . . .	*Ōmang emhālā.*
Dregs . . .	*Tsütse.*
Dress (put on the upper cloth) . . .	*Sōkthetālā.*
Dress (put on the lower cloth) . . .	*Mpenscüekātālā.*
Dress (one's self) . .	*Ōscü mpenālā.*
Dress (another) . .	*Ōscü mpentōkālā.*
Dried up (as a stream) .	*Ōtchhü hngāchecho.*
Drink . . .	*Yūālā.*
Drive . . .	*Vamālā.*
Drive down (as a stake) .	*Eshenālā.*
Drive away, off . .	*Phānisiāla.*
Drop . . .	*Enūngālā.*
Drop (as water) . .	*Lenchōālā.*
Drove . . .	*Khōlōk, tsaten, ten.*

Drown . . . *Ehratsangā.*
Drowsy, to be . . *Yingwhālā, engwālā.*
Drum . . . *Sōnkōng.*
Drunk . . . *Khinōā, ekhiōnā.*
Drunkard . . . *Khinōkhangā.*
Dry . . . *Ekhyang.*
Dry (by the fire) . . *Ehōālā, khyangtōkalā.*
Dry (put out to dry) . *Phikāchiālā.*
Dry up (as a stream) . *Hngāchetālā.*
Duck . . . *Pōtāk.*
Dull . . . *Sesetō.*
Dumb . . . *Eyim.*
Dung . . . *Ōchü.*
Durable . . . *Enhyākā vām, enkyākātsütsān.*
Dusk . . . *Mangsāthang.*
Dust . . . *Khürr.*
Dwarf . . . *Ōmōpvū, rāntāmōchū, lōkōphūtiro, lōkōnyāṉhngwo.*
Dwell . . . *Vānālā.*
Dwelling-place . . *Evāmpheṉ.*
Dye . . . *Ehrü, nünghe.*
Dysentery . . . *Phyōtsangā, echeṉ, phyōtātā.*
Each . . . *Lāngā.*
Each other . . . *Ōnichi, ōniōni.*
Ear . . . *Ennō.*
Ear (auditory canal) . *Ennōkhū.*
Ear (lobe) . . . *Nōmang.*
Ear (hole, for ornaments) . *Ennōvecho.*
Earring . . . *Norr, norri* (made of fine brass coiled like a watch spring).
Earring . . . *Mārōngpen, ōrūng* (made of coloured goat's hair).
Earring . . . *Kōngkā, yempezu.*
Early . . . *Hnyāzangenā, nyāpā* (4 to 5 o'clock).
Earth (world) . . . *Limhātzhū.*
Earth (ground) . . *Ōchōā.*
Earthquake . . . *Ndrū enyōkā.*
East . . . *Engichirophemwe.*
Eastern . . . *Engichiropemwe.*
Easy . . . *Elāshāsā, elakā, n-khang ntsākā.*
Eat . . . *Tsōālā.*
Eatables . . . *Etsōyū, tsopheṉ epheṉ.*

Eaten . . . *Tsöchākā.*
Eaves . . . *Shuwo.*
Echo . . . *Ōwōn, zökātā.*
Edifice . . . *Ōki.*
Effulgent . . . *Etāngrātsangā.*
Effigy . . . *Kyōŋ shancho, kyōṇ lyūcho.*
Egg . . . *Hōno etchhü.*
Egg-plant . . . *Khōnchyū.*
Eight . . . *Tizā.*
Eighteen . . . *Tāro sü tizā.*
Eighty . . . *Ekhātizā, zāro.*
Elbow . . . *Khechü, khetshü.*
Eldest . . . *Erāmō, pökteмōchi.*
Elephant . . . *Sotsü.*
Elsewhere . . . *Thāmphōe.*
Embankment . . . *Epi.*
Embrace . . . *Khānyātālā.*
Employment . . . *Nsündrū.*
Empty . . . *Echang, nyūhā n-chü.*
Encircle . . . *Haiyātālā.*
Enclose . . . *Epiālā, hālā.*
End . . . *Ōchō, kurr.*
Endless . . . *Ōchō, kurr n-ni. Ōchamm n-ni* (limitless).
Enduring . . . *Enhyākā.*
Enemy . . . *Ōrrü.*
Enough, it is . . . *Tetsōā.*
Enquire . . . *Engālā.*
Enslave . . . *Vangālā.*
Enter . . . *Thri yiālā, tāchūngi yiālā.*
Enter (put in) . . *Thechiālā.*
Entire . . . *Ekāni, sāni, meyo.*
Entire (whole) . . *Metāmeyo* (as the whole village).
Entirely . . . *Kān* (affixed to verbal root).
Entrails . . . *Errū. mmā.*
Entrance . . . *Kipang.*
Envious . . . *N-zehngtā, n-khyngtā.*
Equal . . . *Khiti, myāntaktakā* (even).
Erect . . . *Saksaktō, ntsā.*
Escape . . . *'Tsānālā.*
Espouse . . . *Sōāvāntōkālā.*
Eternal . . . *Etchhūhā n-chü, epōhāmpōk.*

Evacuate . . . *Pyōālā.*
Even (level), *adj.* . . *Myānā.*
Even . . . *Hā* (also), *khiti* (exact).
Evening . . . *Milāni.*
Ever . . . *Kōthanghā.*
Every . . . *Lāngā.*
Everyone . . . *Tsak tsakn̲ā, nchyū nchyūnā.*
Everywhere . . . *Metā ākūā, metātsü.*
Every little thing . . *Ntamōmpā.*
Every other day . . *Nchōkā chasi nchōkā.*
Everything . . . *Thārāpvūro, ōmpā, hālān̲gtō, hetōpvū.*
Evil . . . *M-mho.*
Exactly . . . *Penā, epen̲* (fully).
Exact . . . *Ōtscōtsco, myanchākā, khiti.*
Exact (as of weight) . *Ekhyng, khiti.*
Examine . . . *Ntamho zetālā, mhōm mhōnā zetālā.*
Excellent . . . *Tangto mhōnā.*
Excess . . . *Īyākā.*
Excessive . . . *Yākā, tāchōā.*
Exchange . . . *Tōngtālā, n-nitālā.*
Expel . . . *Hōmphōe phānchōkchisiālā.*
Expel (banish) . . *Ekami siālā, phānisiālā.*
Expel (breath) . . *Ephichiālā, ehāchiālā.*
Expense . . . *Ezān̲.*
Explain . . . *Ntsūtōkālā.*
Expose . . . *Echiālā.*
Extinguish . . . *Mhetōkālā.*
Eye . . . *Ōmhyek.*
Eye-ball . . . *Mhyektsang.*
Eye-brow . . . *Mhyekōn̲, ōmhyekmhū.*
Eye-lash . . . *Mhyek tshān̲.*
Eye-lid . . . *Mhyek fhū.*
Eye-sore . . . *Eze m-mho.*

F

Face . . . *Ōmhā.*
Face to face . . . *Ōmhālo renkātā.*
Fade . . . *Chōiyālā* (with name of the color).
Faint . . . *Zānghālā.*
Fair (beautiful) . . *Eze hn̓gā, eze mhōnā.*

Fair (weather) . . *Tsanglā mhōna.*
Fall down . . . *Enūngālā, ekhangāla.*
Fall down (as a tree) . *Eyālā.*
Fall down (as water) . *Zānchōālā, ephyā chōālā.*
Fall down (out of bundle) *Esōkrālā, zānālā.*
Fall down (across) . *Mphiwō eyālā, ehrapzisiālā, thronzisiālā, chüzisiālā.*
False . . . *Echang, n-tsā.*
Falsehood . . . *Echang.*
Family . . . *Wōpān* (the people of one house).
Family . . . *Onthruhru, wōmpā.*
Family (generations, descendants) . . . *Ōtsōeri.*
Famine . . . *Khangā.*
Fan, *n* . . . *Savendro, vemphen.*
Fan, *v* . . . *Vemphiālā.*
Far . . . *Ekōni, lānkōnā, elam kōnā.*
Far-sighted . . . *Ōmhyek ntsenā.*
Farther . . . *Ekōmo.*
Fast (secure) . . *Rārangi, mhōnā, ekhyō.*
Fast (rapid) . . . *Setōā, ekhiolākā, ekhyūngā.*
Fasten . . . *Shenālā, shenkātālā, khānālā.*
Fasten (bind to a tree or stake) . . . *Ōtōng khangkātālā.*
Fastener . . . *Ntsüphen.*
Fat . . . *Peletā.*
Father . . . *Pō, ōpō.*
Father-in-law . . *Ōmō.*
Father (grand) . . *Ōmōtsü, ōmōtsü.*
Father (great grand) . *Pyamtsi, mōtsi.*
Fatigue . . . *Mōkthātā.*
Fault . . . *Phiōphi.*
Faultless . . . *Phiōphi n-ni.*
Favour . . . *Nzānā.*
Favour (in a law-suit) . *Ōyilo theyālā.*
Fear . . . *Khyūtālā.*
Fearful . . . *Ndrensapkhangā, kāphyōkā.*
Fearless . . . *Ntihā ekyū n-ni.*
Feast (to make) . . *Khyōālā, ōshō lyūālā.*
Feather (long tail feather) *Eli, eyū.*
Feather . . . *Ōhm.*
Feeble . . . *Etho n-chü.*

Feed (eat, graze) . . *Tsōālā.*
Feed (to give food to) . *Tsōtōkālā.*
Feel (badly, sad) . . *Nüngrālā, nangrālā.*
Feel (to touch) . . *Ephiā phiālā.*
Feet . . . *Mpho.*
Fell (trees) . . . *Tāni eyālōkālā.*
Female . . . *Elüē, ōkhö*
Fence . . . *Pāhrr, pāhri.*
Fern . . . *Tscangōno.*
Fertile . . . *Lōkōtsō.*
Festival . . . *Ōshō, emū.*
Festival, to make . . *Ōsho lyūālā.*
Fetch . . . *Hāṇai yiālā, pensi yiālā.*
Fever . . . *Liōrā, rā.*
Fever, to have . . *Liōrā rālā.*
Few . . . *Etchakāro, terrāro.*
Fibula . . . *Nüng kurr, nüng kurrü.*
Fife . . . *Philūli, phiyūyū.*
Fifteen . . . *Tāro sü mūngo.*
Fifty . . . *Tiingyā.*
Fig . . . *Zōwōchi, tsüpekhi, khyoyōkhi.*
Fight . . . *Ōrrü tsōālā, sātālā, ōrrüchentālā.*
Fight (as cattle) . . *Shāngtālā.*
Fight (as horses) . . *Epātālā.*
Fight (as dogs) . . *Rōtālā.*
Fight (as birds) . . *Ntsütālā.*
Fight (as children) . . *Khōntālā.*
Fight (as fowls) . . *Nōktālā, ntsütālā.*
Fight (as swine) . . *Echamtālā.*
Fill . . . *Phyangālā.*
Fin . . . *Ngotsū, chōkū.*
Find . . . *Yānchetālā, mhūngālā.*
Fine (as of wood) . . *Vārōā, tsārōā.*
Fine (as of cloth) . . *Nnaksankerrā.*
Finger . . . *Yingdro.*
Finger (little) . . . *Yingtamo.*
Finger (middle) . . *Yingnūngo.*
Finger (first) . . . *Ying tsüwo.*
Finger nail . . . *Yingkyep.*
Finish . . . . *Sā, kāṉsā* (affixed to verbal root).
Fire, *n.* . . . *Ōmi.*
Fire, *v.* . . . *Thenālā, rōngālā.*

Fire (a gun) . . .	*Khiālā, thiālā.*
Firefly . . .	*Ōrru sāsāpvü.*
Firewood . . .	*Ōtscang.*
Fireplace . . .	*Mitsōphen, nchakūwe.*
Firm . . .	*Chūng chūngtō, renā.*
Firmament . . .	*Ōyāki.*
First . . .	*Yitemo, ōvūngo, tem* or *ten* affixed to verb.
First-born . . .	*Pōktemōchü.*
Fish . . .	*Ōngo.*
Fisherman . . .	*Phyōkālo ewe, ōngō eye.*
Fish-hook . . .	*Ōngo ōkhū, ngokhū.*
Fish-net . . .	*Ngotsōphen.*
Fishing-rod . . .	*Ngokhūtōng.*
Fissure . . .	*Ekak.*
Fist . . .	*Khezam.*
Fix . . .	*Mhōnā lyūā.*
Flag . . .	*Simyō.*
Flame, *n.* . . .	*Ōmi ekhi.*
Flame, *v.* . . .	*Ōmi ekhiālā.*
Flat (of ground) . .	*Haiyi.*
Flat (of stones) . .	*Epyākā.*
Flatulent . . .	*Vechiā.*
Flea . . .	*Tezü.*
Flee . . .	*Tsānālā, tsānai yiālā.*
Fleet . . .	*Lelapā, ekhyangā.*
Flesh . . .	*Ōsō.*
Float (in water) . .	*Phūphiālā, nkhikāro vānālā.*
Float (in the air) . .	*Vēnai yālā, pūngai yālā.*
Flock . . .	*Ōten.*
Floor . . .	*Tāpvwi.*
Flour . . .	*Ōhm.*
Flow . . .	*Phyōnālā, chōiyālā.*
Flower, *n.* . . .	*Therā.*
Flute . . .	*Phiyüyü.*
Fly, *v.* . . .	*Phyai yālā.*
Fly, *n.* . . .	*Penō.*
Fly, sand . . .	*Penchakāro.*
Foam . . .	*Ōtchhü mpen.*
Foe . . .	*Ōrrū, ōri.*
Fog . . .	*Emhentzhü.*
Fold . . .	*Chapālā.*

Follow	*Phānālā, etāngālā, silāmi-wālā.*
Follow (close on behind)	*Ōscülo erikātā phānālā.*
Fool	*Nyūhā n-tsü kyōn̲.*
Foolish	*Nyūhā n-tsü.*
Foot	*Mpo, chōmpo.*
Foot (base)	*Nthang, ōchō.*
Foot-print Foot-step	*Khōsü.*
For	*Etchi, etchü, etscōnā ;* affixes *ō, lō.*
Forbid	*Siātālā.*
Force	*Tōkālā* (causative affix).
Forcibly	*Rrechō.*
Ford	*Pōfü khyangkōkā.*
Forefathers	*Pyamtsümōtsi.*
Forefinger	*Yingtsüo.*
Forehead	*Ōtōn̲.*
Foreigner	*Yāmpōe, thāmphōe.*
Forenoon	*Nshü n-tanghā*
Foreskin	*Zung-fhu.*
Forest	*Erānī, enūng.*
Forge, *n.*	*Yōnchōki.*
Forge, *v.*	*Ephiātālā.*
Forget	*Mhechōālā.*
Forgotten	*Mhechākā.*
Fork	*Esham.*
Former	*Ehemwōchi, ōvūngōchü.*
Formerly	*Nūngkōlō, ngkōlō* (a long time).
Formerly	*Ōsī* (a short time).
Forsake	*Süsü yiālā.*
Fort (and fortification)	*Kherāsü.*
Forty	*Züro.*
Fortunate	*Mmhā.*
Found	*Yānchetā, yānchecho.*
Fortune, to tell	*Okhe thenālā.*
Fowl	*Hōnō.*
Fowler	*Wōro echhi.*
Four	*Mezü.*
Fourteen	*Tāro sü mezü.*
Fragrance	*Ōhram.*
Fragrant	*Ōhramerā, ōhrameriā.*
Free	*N-vang.*
Frequently	*Nsānsam.*

Friend . . . *Ōkamo, ōchenī, ōshōm.*
Frighten . . . *Ekhentōkālā.*
Fringe . . . *Scūcham.*
Frog . . . *Ōvū.*
From . . . *Nā*(affixed to nouns).
From that time . . . *Chisīchō.*
From, to (from village to village, is a short distance) . . . *Yāṉyiṉ enghyānō.*
Front . . . *Mhātūng, mhātūngi, ōvūng.*
Front-room . . . *Sōntōlī.*
Front-yard . . . *Hōnkūwe.*
Froth . . . *Otchhü elā, otchhü etsü.*
Fruit-stone . . . *Tsangthitsang.*
Fruitless . . . *Tsangthi m-pā.*
Fuel . . . *Ōtsang.*
Full . . . *Phyangā.*
Fun . . . *Ngangōtā.*
Fur . . . *Ohm, ōtsāṉ.*
Future (another time) . *Thāmpōthang.*

G

Gadfly . . . *Sōpeṉ.*
Gain . . . *Rāṉgkātā, kāk.*
Gall . . . *Ōtscü, ōmōtscü.*
Gallop . . . *Tsōkā yiālā.*
Gamble . . . *Fhufho nrōktālā.*
Gambol . . . *Ekhiōlākālā.*
Gape . . . *Hōmhuālā, hōmhālā.*
Garden . . . *Pāhrr.*
Gardener . . . *Pāhrr echoṉ.*
Garlic . . . *Lāsen.*
Gate . . . *Khāmpheṉ.*
Gate (village) . . . *Pikhū khāmpheṉ.*
Gather . . . *Khiōthrōālā, nshātsōi vātālā.*
Gather up (as cloth in the hand). *Sārthrūālā.*
Gather (as clouds) . . *Rōmālā.*
Gaze . . . *Zetālā, ngāngā zetālā.*
Generation (family) . *Ōtsōeri.*
Gentle . . . *M-hārōk.*

Get . . .	*Hngālā, khiālā.*
Get out of the way . .	*Nkā chiālā.*
"Ghat" . . .	*Erū.*
Gift . . .	*Ōthāṉ.*
Ginger . . .	*Ōsāng.*
Girdle . . .	*Erūlōtsenthepeṉ.*
Girl . . .	*Elūē roro.*
Give . . .	*Piālā.*
Gizzard . . .	*Mmā.*
Glad . . .	*Emāthātā.*
Glass . . .	*Ōmhā chāmphen.*
Gloomy . . .	*Yimā* (*See* Lowery).
Glorify . . .	*Tsūpōtōkālā, ekhūngtokālā.*
Glow-worm . . .	*Ōrü sāsāpvū.*
Glue . . .	*Oni.*
Glutton . . .	*Ōpang tangotsakshiā.*
Gnat . . .	*Tsōkhüpencham.*
Gnaw . . .	*Nkōkālā.*
Go . . .	*Wōālā, yiālā, wālā.*
Go around . . .	*Thrrüphyalā.*
Go down . . .	*Chōwālā, chōi-iyālā.*
Go down (as a swelling) .	*Sāpālā.*
Go down (as the arm of a balance).	*Etāngāḷā.*
Go in . . .	*Thrōi yiālā, thre yiālā.*
Go up . . .	*Chūngwālā, chūng yiālā.*
Go up (as a balance) .	*Nkanālā.*
Go out . . .	*Chī yiālā.*
Go out (as a fire) . .	*Mhetālā.*
Goat . . .	*Nyānyā.*
Goat hair (dyed red) .	*Ōrūng.*
God . . .	*Yihōvā.*
God (supreme spirits, one evil and one good).	*Potsōwō.*
God (river-god) . .	*Tsangdhram.*
God (forest-god) . .	*Nungkam, Lunkamo.*
Goitre . . .	*Ngūtyū.*
Golaghat . . .	*Kūlai.*
Gong . . .	*Ōphiang, kāngkāngū.*
Good . . .	*Mhōnā, mhōm.*
Goods . . .	*Kikhio mokhiō, kikhyō ni khiyō, ōkī leyi.*

Goose . . .	*Hāngū.*
Gore, *v.* . . .	*Chentālā.*
Gourd . . .	*Lefū.*
Grab . . .	*Eyā chōi khiālā.*
Grace . . .	*Nsāṉ.*
Gradually . . .	*Echamchamnā.*
Granary . . .	*Ōscoṉ.*
Grand-daughter . .	*Ōsüwo.*
Grand-father . . .	*Ōmōtsü.*
Grand-mother . .	*Ōtsü, ōtzü.*
Grand-son . . .	*Ōtsōerri, ōrüwō.*
Grand-parents . .	*Piamtsū mōtsü.*
Grasp . . .	*Hramālā, rhamālā, penālā.*
Grass . . .	*Lōmo, ōchāk, erōyō.*
Grasshopper . . .	*Hāpvūro.*
Gratis . . .	*Tācho.*
Grave . . .	*Ōlap, ōkab, ōkhap.*
Graze . . .	*Erō rangi tsōālā, ōtsāk tsōālā.*
Grease . . .	*Ekhū.*
Great . . .	*Tsapō.*
Greedy . . .	*Ōpang tsakshükhangā.* *Ōpang ekhan khangā.*
Green (fresh) . .	*Enīro, eshü.*
Green (partly) . .	*Mhen shüshāk.*
Green (colour) . .	*Thōwōnā.*
Grief . . .	*Nūngrāthātā.*
Grind (as grain) . .	*Enhyākālā.*
Grind (to sharpen) . .	*Ehetālā, phyākālā.*
Grind-stone . . .	*Mōrāk, lepōk phiākpheṉ, lepōk ehepheṉ.*
Groan . . .	*Drrālā.*
Ground . . .	*Ōchhōṉ, lōko.*
Ground-pine . . .	*Lōko samcho.*
Grow (in length) . .	*Rāngkātālā.*
Grow (in volume) . .	*Tsakātālā.*
Grow out (as horn or nails).	*Shūngwālā.*
Grow up (sprout) . .	*Shūngwātchi rōālā.*
Growl . . .	*Nyeṉālā.*
Grub . . .	*Chōrō.*
Grumble . . .	*Ethō chākālā.*
Guard . . .	*Rārangi hnyākā vānālā, ōlāṉ samālā.*
Guardian . . .	*Suphichecho, ōpōro.*

Guest . . . *Ōki müngchōwōchi, ōki vā̱n yiäwōchi.*
Guide, *v.* . . . *Ōlā̱n echhiālā.*
Guide (lead), *v.* . . *Edrālā.*
Guide, *n.* . . . *Ōlā̱n echhūwōchü.*
Guitar . . . *Khūphe̱n.*
Gulp . . . *Tsōmālā.*
Gum . . . *Tsütse.*
Gun . . . *Tsangi, tsange.*
Gunpowder . . . *Khorr.*
Gutter . . . *Shūwōmyenthe.*

H

Habit (custom) . . *Shükhü.*
Habit . . . *Etsōphyō.*
Habitation . . . *Vāmphe̱n.*
Hail (stone), *n.* . . *Shehrü, sherrü.*
Hail, *v.* . . . *Sehrü chōālā, sherrü chōālā.*
Hair (of the head) . . *Ōtsa̱n.*
Hair (of the body) . . *Ōhm.*
Half . . . *Pōko.*
Halfway . . . *Ōlā̱n tchüse, ōlā̱n ōnūngo, ōlā̱n tālālo.*
Halve . . . *Enī nūngsōālā, phangsōālā.*
Hand . . . *Ōkhe.*
Handle . . . *Ntsap, ramhāphe̱n, hramhāphe̱n.*
Hang (*intrans.*) . . *Khyākthe chiālā.*
Hang (*trans.*) . . . *Khyākthātālā.*
Hang up (as a flag) . . *Tōnālā.*
Hang down . . *Zōnchōālā.*
Hang (as fruit on a tree) . *Ethiālā.*
Hang up (on a hook or nail) *Yīkālā.*
Hang (over a line) . . *Yisī vātālā.*
Happy . . . *Emāthātā.*
Hard . . . *Khangā, rok rok.*
Hare-lip . . . *Mefū m-pā̱n.*
Harvest, *v.* . . . *Ōlī rātālā, ōli rālā.*
Harvest time . . . *Yerupūngo, ōlī rāthang.*
Hat . . . *Kive̱n, khiko, kikho.*
Hatch . . . *Hōno khechōālā.*
Hate . . . *Nlamālā.*
"Hatigoria" . . . *Chhüm.*
Have . . . *Vānā, liā, chhūā.*
Hawk . . . *Mangshiro.*

He . . . *Shī, chī.*
Head . . . *Kurr.*
Headache . . . *Kūrrī nökhangā, kurrīvāvapā.*
Heal . . . *Pōālā, tscenchetālā, tānang chetālā.*
Healthy . . . *Mhā.*
Heap . . . *Khōlōk, nsha.*
Hear . . . *Zōālō, engālā, söthrakātālā, söhrākā.*
Heart . . . *Lampam.*
Hearth . . . *Ōmī tsōpheṉ.*
Heat . . . *Lammālā.*
Heave . . . *Echam kāchiālā.*
Heaven . . . *Potsōwō.*
Heavy . . . *Khekhe, myangā.*
Heel . . . *Nkhōng.*
Heifer . . . *Māngsü lammī.*
Height . . . *Ntsoṉ.*
Help . . . *Khyüālā.*
Helpless . . . *Ethō n-chhü.*
Hem . . . *Ōscu ekham, ōscü evü.*
Hen . . . *Hānkhō.*
Hence . . . *Hellōnā.*
Henceforth . . . *Hīsīcho.*
Hen roost . . . *Hōno ḥānki, hōno khyingpheṉ.*
Her . . . *Shi.*
Herd, *n.* . . . *Tsüteṉ, teṉ.*
Herd, *v.* . . . *Ekamālā.*
Herdsman . . . *Māngsü ekam.*
Here . . . *Hello.*
Hereafter . . . *Hisi, ōkhānāti.*
Here and there . . *Ōlo-ōlo.*
Hew . . . *Tanālā, nangālā.*
Hiccough . . . *Nkhichī.*
Hide, *v.* . . . *Mphōā yiālā, mpōi vātālā.*
Hide, *n.* . . . *Ōfhü.*
High . . . *Ntsōnā, ōyākī.*
Highway . . . *Pōkilāṉ.*
Hill . . . *Yōntōngdro.*
Him . . . *Shī.*
Himself . . . *Ōmō, ōmōmō, mpōpō.*
Hinder . . . *Khetsālā.*
Hip . . . *Khāngkheṉ.*
His . . . *Mpō, shī.*

English	Lhota
Hiss	*Shūshiālā.*
Hit	*Tamālā, ekhōkātālā, tāpālā.*
Hither	*Épī, hepī.*
Hive	*Ōtsāk vāmphen̲, ōtsāk pho.*
Hoe, *v.*	*Thrōnālā.*
Hoe, *n*	*Chōkchhü, kōperāng.*
Hog	*Wōko.*
Hog-trough	*Vekhū.*
Hoist	*Tōnālā.*
Hold	*Hramālā, penālā.*
Hold (contain)	*Thetālā.*
Hold (in arms)	*Sōālā, echamālā.*
Hold out (the arms)	*Ōkhe ntīchetālā, ōkhe rūchiālā.*
Hole	*Epo, ōkū.*
Hollow	*Rāngkū.*
Honest	*Ntsen̲, ntsā.*
Honey	*Tsāk etchhü, tsākītzü.*
Honey-comb	*Tsākpo.*
Hoof	*Nōngkhū, nkhū.*
Hook, *n.*	*Ōyāk.*
Hook, *v.*	*Shūngālā.*
Hop	*Tsōkā tsānālā, tsōkālā.*
Horn	*Echhü, etshü.*
Hornet	*Rōngwe, nangtchhü. tsāktsü.*
Horse	*Korr.*
Hot	*Tscōā, tscōshāshāpā.*
Hot-water	*Chhüshen̲, chhülam.*
Hot-season	*Yichen̲, yion̲thang, elamō.*
House	*Ōkī.*
House (dhan)	*Ōshōn̲.*
House (very small)	*Kitōkro.*
House	*Champā* (where persons sleep for a night, who have been bitten by a tiger).
Household	*Ōpvwī.*
House fly	*Penō.*
Hospitable	*Ōyān̲tānang.*
Hospital	*Pīrap morom kī.*
Hostile	*Ōrrütav.*
How	*Kōtōli*
Howl	*Thrükīāpālā.*
How many	*Kōtātā.*
How much	*Kōtātā.*

How often . . .	*Kōtāthang.*
Hundred . . .	*Nzoā.*
Hunger . . .	*Wōntōn.*
Hungry . . .	*Wōntōntsangā.*
Hunt . . .	*Ōsōkōpō īyālā, ōsōkhilo iyālā.*
Hunter . . .	*Ōsōkhīlewe, ōsōkōpōewe.*
Hurl . . .	*Ephiā tsangālā.*
Hurricane . . .	*Tsangrompeṉ.*
Hurry . . .	*Ekhiāpā yiā, süto tsütōnāyiā, ndrā yiā seto yiā, ekhyangā īyā.*
Hurt . . .	*Nōkhangā* (with verb).
Husband . . .	*Ōrāpvū, ōki khamō.*
Husk, *n.* . . .	*Ōfū.*
Husk, *v.* . . .	*Ōfū rāki siālā, ōfū rākālā.*
Hypocrite . . .	*Tāchō ephyōwe.*

I

I . . .	*Ā, ai, aiyō, ākhā.*
Idiot . . .	*N-tsü kyōṉ.*
Idle . . .	*N-tyūlāhā mpāng.*
Idler . . .	*Ōlām pangū.*
If . . .	*Nā* (verbal affix).
Ignite . . .	*Mpōng kātālā, nchang kātālā.*
Ignorant . . .	*N-tsü, n-tsi.*
Ill . . .	*Rāthātā, pirapthātā, nōchōnōrā ōtsako enōmpāpā.*
Ill-fortune . . .	*Sakhyang n-ni*
Image . . .	*Ōmōṉ.*
Immediately . . .	*Ndrā, setōā.*
Immodest . . .	*N-yikrā.*
Immerse . . .	*Chūngthechiala.*
Immortal . . .	*Kōthanghā n-tchhü.*
Impassable . . .	*Menzā, meṉchākā, n-khyngkōk.*
Impatient . . .	*Kārang.*
Imprison, *v.* . . .	*Vangālā.*
In . . .	*Tāchūngi, ōnūngi* (*lō* and *i* affixed to nouns).
In company with . .	*Pānā, nzō.*
Indeed (truly) . .	*Ōtscōtscō.*
Increase . . .	*Khyōngkātā yiālā, khyōngkātālā, khichetālā.*

Increase (in size, grow) . *Rāngākātālā.*
Increase (in length) . *Sakātālā.*
Incredible . . . *N-nangtsü.*
Indian-corn . . . *Tsangōndhro.*
Indigent . . . *Ezapthātā, yāntse.*
Indisposed . . . *Ōrüchākā.*
Industrious . . . *Kōntsangā, lamkhyingā.*
Infancy . . . *Ngārothang.*
Infant . . . *Ngāro.*
Infanticide . . . *Ngāro köcho, ngaro ephiācho.*
In front . . . *Mhātüngī.*
Inhabit . . . *Vānālā.*
Inhabitant . . . *Evāmōchü.*
Inhale . . . *Enghüālā, enghālā.*
Ink . . . *Kākōtzü, kākōtchhü.*
Ink-stand . . . *Kākōtzü thephen.*
Innumerable . . . *N-khākhangkōk.*
Inquire . . . *Engālā.*
Insane . . . *Zeven, zavai.*
Insect . . . *Ōrā.*
Insert . . . *Thevātālā.*
Inside . . . *Tāchüngi, ōchüngi.*
Instantly . . . *Nthāngā.*
Instead of . . . *Thōng.*
Instruct . . . *Shīkālā.*
Insufficient . . . *Zānkhangā, zāngkhangā.*
Interest, *n.* . . . *Chākche, rāngke.*
Interpret . . . *Ōyī elōnyālā, ōyī lamphenyālā.*
Interpreter . . . *Lamphen, ōyī elon.*
Intestines . . . *Errü.*
Into . . . *Tāchüngi, onüngwe.*
Intoxicate . . . *Kīnōlōkālā.*
Invest . . . *Sōkthetālā.*
Invite . . . *Tsālā.*
Iron . . . *Yōngchāk, yōnchāk.*
Is . . . *Liā, vānā, chiā.*
Island . . . *Otchhü lüngwi ōchōn eliwōchü.*
Is not . . . *N-lī, n-nī, m-mā.*
Itch, *v.* . . . *Entkākālā.*
Itch, *n.* . . . *Enthākā.*
Itself . . . *Ōmōmōn.*
Ivory . . . *Sōtsü hō, sōtzü hō.*

J

Jabber . . . *Ōyi khyōng khangālā, ōyi pōrākātā.*
Jacket . . . *Sōkthescü etchakāro.*
Jail . . . *Evangkī.*
Jaw . . . *Ōkan, ōkandrrü.*
Jew's-harp . . . *Khūkhiang, khūchang.*
Join . . . *Echūngtālā, wōtālā.*
Join (as two streams) . *Errü hrütālā, phyōnsütālā.*
Joint (of a plant) . . *Ōlōn.*
Joint (of the body) . . *Chüngkū.*
Joy . . . *Emā.*
Joyful . . . *Emāthā, emātsāngā.*
Judge, *v.* . . . *Ōnūngo ephyōālā.*
Juice . . . *Ōtchhü.*
Jump . . . *Tsōkālā.*
Jungle . . . *Ōrā, rōmhōnī.*
Jungly . . . *Zangā.*
Jungle-fowl . . . *Wōro.*

K

Keep . . . *Vātālā.*
Keep (tend) . . . *Ekamālā.*
Keep (in confinement) . *Vangālā.*
Kettle . . . *Lampen, shempen.*
Key . . . *Chōnchephen, nyāchephen.*
"Khel" . . . *Eyangko, kīthāng.*
Kick (with the toe of foot) *Nshiālā.*
Kick . . . *Epāphiālā, nkānphiālā.*
Kick (with the sole of foot) *Echūtālā.*
Kick (as horses) . . *Epāthātā.*
Kid . . . *Nyānyāro.*
Kidneys . . . *Sepyek.*
Kill . . . *Sāthātālā, nangthātālā, tchhitōkālā.*
Kill (by pounding) . . *Sāthātālā, sātsangālā.*
Kill (by cutting off head) . *Kurr wōnālā.*
Kill (by cutting the throat) *Hōtsangālā.*
Kill (by spearing) . . *Chenālā.*
Kilt . . . *Erako, ryūye.*
Kilt (Āngāmi) . . *Sühram.*
Kind, *n.* . . . *Tuv* (affix).

Kindle (a fire) . . *Ōmi-tsōālā.*
Kindness . . . *Nzāṉ.*
Kiss . . . *Chōnchiālā.*
Kitchen . . . *Ōtsü rüpheṉ.*
Kitten . . . *Ōlyūrōro, ōyūrōro.*
Knee . . . *Nkho.*
Kneel . . . *Khōktsenālā.*
Knife (large) . . . *Yōnthā.*
Knife . . . *Lepōk.*
Knife (pocket) . . *Lepōkro.*
Knock . . . *Chemphiālā, kōkōkālā.*
Knot, *n.* . . . *Ntscü.*
Knot, *v.* . . . *Ntscüālā.*
Know . . . *Ntsiālā.*
Knowledge . . . *Ōkiāk.*
Knuckle . . . *Khemhyek.*
"Koni dhán" . . . *Ōteṉ.*

L

Labour, *n.* . . . *Nsündrü, elapā.*
Labour, *v.* . . . *Nsǖndrrūelā, elapālā.*
Lad . . . *Nūngōr, erānkam.*
Ladder . . . *Pōpā.*
Lady . . . *Etsielōe.*
Lake . . . *Wǖzǖ.*
Lamb . . . *Kātsōro.*
Lame . . . *Ōchōechāng.*
Lamp . . . *Ōmi tsōpheṉ, ōmikipheṉ.*
Land (country) . . *Metā, metāmeyo.*
Land (not water) . . *Lōko.*
Land-mark . . . *Errǖ.*
Landslip . . . *Lōko mencho.*
Language . . . *Ōyi.*
Lantern . . . *Thangdrāchōngpheṉ.*
Lap (with tongue, *v.*) . *Myākālā.*
Lap, take on . . *Ōphilo ekāchiālā.*
Lap . . . *Ōphi.*
Lard . . . *Wōko-so ekhǖ, wōko so ethǖ.*
Large . . . *Tsapō, tsakhangā.*
Large . . . *Pvū* (*kyōṉpvū*, large man).
Large . . . *Tsū* (*ōvāntsǖ*, large village).

Larger . . .	*Tsapōwōchü, tsapōwōchi.*
Last . . .	*Silāmō.*
Late . . .	*Nshutāngā, enhyākā.*
Latter . . .	*Silāmōchü. silāmwōchü.*
Laugh . . .	*Emāthātālā.*
Laugh—laughter . .	*Emāthā.*
Lavender . . .	*Tōwōnā.*
Law . . .	*Eshakhū.*
Lawless . . .	*Eshakhū n-khi.*
Lawsuit . . .	*Ōyitsōtuwochi*
Lay . . .	*Vātālā.*
Lay (eggs) . . .	*Etchiālā.*
Lay down . . .	*Eraki vānālā.*
Layer . . .	*Ōren.*
Lazy . . .	*Rūchākhangā, rūchākā, lōthiā, rākzā.*
Lead, *v.* . . .	*Süsütsātā, süālā, siālā.*
Lead, *n.* . . .	*Phyōntsü.*
Leaf . . .	*Ōwō, lōmo.*
Leaf (plantain leaf) . .	*Ōyo.*
Leak . . .	*Sōālā, echōthetālā.*
Lean . . .	*Kūrrtsangā, kwūrritsangā.*
Lean (flesh) . . .	*Ōzü.*
Lean, *v.* . . .	*Enhikātālā.*
Leap . . .	*Chōkpiālā.*
Leap down . . .	*Tsōkchōālā.*
Leather . . .	*Sōfū.*
Leave . . .	*Süsi yiālā, siālā.*
Leech (land) . . .	*Evān.*
Leech (water) . .	*Nnā, nlā.*
Left, *v.* . . .	*Vāchichākā.*
Left-hand . . .	*Ōkhē-āyiwe.*
Left-side . . .	*Ōyiwe.*
Leg . . .	*Ōchō.*
Leg (above knee) . .	*Ōphi, ndrā.*
Leg (to a stand, table, &c.)	*Chenkiā.*
Lemon . . .	*Tsāmpen.*
Length . . .	*Sapō.*
Lengthen . . .	*Sapō lyūālā.*
Lengthwise . . .	*Thōngāwō.*
Lenient . . .	*Ōtsākō ese mazzu.*
Leopard . . .	*Mhorr terrūwō.*
Let . . .	*Tōkā* (verbal affix).

English	Lhota
Let go	*Vāchiālā.*
Letter	*Kāko.*
Level	*Myānā, haiyī.*
Liar	*Echang-ephyōe, tācho ephyōe, ōyi n-tsā kyon.*
Lick	*Myākālā.*
Lid	*Hlaphen.*
Lie, *v.*	*Echang phyōālā.*
Lie, *n.*	*Echang.*
Lie down	*Eraki vānālā, yipālā.*
Lie (in wait)	*Rāvānālā.*
Lie (on back)	*Nthikārō yipālā.*
Lie (on side)	*Tsātsōkō yipālā.*
Lie (on belly)	*Nkhammāwō yipālā.*
Life	*Ethak.*
Lift	*Echamālā, esekātālā.*
Light, *n.*	*Tāngtāng.*
Light, *adj.*	*Zakhōā* (not heavy).
Lightens	*Tsanglapālā, nlapālā.*
Like	*Essā* (similar), affix *tuv, khiti, kheti* (equal).
Like, *v.*	*Lammālā, chōkātālā, tsūpōnālā nsāntālā, chūpōnālā, eyiliālā.*
Likely	*Sālā.*
Limb (of a tree)	*Esham, choiyang.*
Lime	*Fhūforōngchō.*
Limit	*Errū, ōtse.*
Limp	*Esōngālā.*
Line, *n.*	*Sangā, sangcho.*
Line (of face or hand)	*Ehrū.*
Line (fishing)	*Ngōkhūzū, ōkhūzū.*
Line (of houses)	*Kīren.*
Line, stand in a	*Renī vānālā* (side by side).
Line, stand in a	*Zatangi vānālā* (one in front of another).
Line, sit in a line side by side.	*Rentā vānālā.*
Link	*Nkōncho.*
Lip	*Menfū.*
Liquor	*Sōkō*
Liquor (strong)	*Zūtchhū.*
Listen	*Engālā.*

Little	*Etchakāro, teraro, echakchakro.*
Little (short)	*Ehnghngdro.*
Little while	*Esangāro.*
Live	*Ekam vānālā, kamā vānālā, kāmālā.*
Liver	*Nten.*
Living	*Ekam.*
Lizzard	*Ōmōndro.*
Lo!	*Zetā.*
Load	*Ōhā.*
Loan, *v.*	*Nōpālā.*
Lock	*Khāmphen.*
Locust	*Kōmūng.*
Lofty	*Elam sīpōā, mpemō ntsōnā, ōyākī.*
Log	*Echōā, ōtōng myi.*
Loins	*Errū.*
Long-lived	*Hārishīā, enhyākā, piphirōngsā.*
Long ago.	*Ngkōlō.*
Long time	*Enhyākā.*
Longer	*Sükuwō, sāpōwo.*
Long	*Sapō, ephiā, ekonī,* (distant).
Look at	*Zetālā, zechiālā.*
Look up	*Zekāchālā.*
Look down	*Zechōchīālā, zetechālā.*
Looking-glass	*Ōmhā chāmphen.*
Loom	*Ōscū takphen.*
Loose	*Tākuā.*
Loosen	*Ephe chiālā, lāmphetālā.*
Lose	*Mōnā siālā.*
Loss	*Epapā, epapvū.*
Lost	*Mōnīchākā.*
Loud	*Ekhiōtō, ekhiō.*
Louse	*Ōhrak.*
Louse (eggs of)	*Hrak tchhü.*
Love	*Chipontālā, lammālā, eyilōtālā.*
Lovely	*Tangto mhōnā, ezehngtsangā.*
Low	*Mmhyemā, nkapi, ōkapi, ennāto.*
Low, *v.*	*Nrōngālā.*
Lower	*Ōkapō.*
Lowery (weather)	*Tsang yimā.*
Luck	*Sükhying.*
Luggage	*Ōhā.*
Lump	*Pamā, khōnūng.*

Lump (of dirt) . . *Changkhōnūng.*
Luncheon . . . *Nshi, nshü.*
Lurk . . . *Mphōā vānālā.*
Lust . . . *Lamm khangā.*
Lustrous . . . *Tsanglapā.*
Lye . . . *Kōrtchhü.*

M

Mad . . . *Zaven̲.*
Mad, *v.* . . . *Khōnālā.*
Maggot . . . *Tepvü, ōrā.*
Maid . . . *Lōrōe, elōe rōro, lōrān̲.*
Maintain . . . *Esaphichetālā.*
Make . . . *Lyüālā.*
Make (fire) . . . *Tscōālā.*
Male (of men) . . *Epüe, pāni.*
Male (of animals) . . *Ōpōng.*
Man . . . *Kyōn̲.*
Man (young married) . *Chāli, chāyi.*
Man (young unmarried) . *Khingdrōe.*
Mane . . . *Ōtscān̲, ōhm.*
Mango . . . *Tsapyüngthi, tsipyüngthi.*
Manhood . . . *Chālithang.*
Manipulate (the body) . *Emephiālā, epiāmphiālā.*
Manure . . . *Ōchü.*
Many . . . *Elam, kōshā.*
Many (so) . . . *Hetātā.*
Many (very) . . . *Ōtscān̲tātā* (as many as the hairs of the head).
Mare . . . *Kōrr ōkō.*
Marigold . . . *Yāntān therā.*
Mark, *v.* . . . *Chethe lüālā, setālā.*
Mark (sign), *n.* . . *Chethe.*
Mark (line) . . . *Secho, sangche.*
Market . . . *Shishōphen̲.*
Marriage (to give in) . *Elōe sōāvāntōkālā.*
Marriage (to ask in) . *Elōe engālā.*
Marry . . . *Elōe sōāvānālā.*
Marsh . . . *Chonchen̲yo, chōnpyaiyü.*
Master . . . *Ōpvwi.*
Mat . . . *Ōphak.*

Match	*Ōmisephen, ōmi nkhyophen.*
Mate	*Ōshōno.*
"Mati Mah"	*Ōsamdhrō.*
Matter	*Chencho.*
Matter (what is the)?	*Niūō tsōchōlā.*
Matting (of bamboo)	*Ōkiam.*
Mature	*Emhe.*
May	*Che, tōku* (verbal affixes).
Me	*Ā.*
Meal	*Ōrrang, eyīngtse.*
Measles	*Nūngzāk.*
Measles, to have	*Nūngzāk shenālā.*
Measure, *v.*	*Kōpe zetālā, etsiālā.*
Measure, *v.*	*Fhūālā.* (See Tables.)
Meat	*Ōso.*
Meat basket	*Sōpap.*
Medicine	*Mazü.*
Mediate	*Ōyi onūngo ephyōā.*
Meet	*Ntōkālā.*
Meet (and return with)	*Eyīlowō.*
Mem sahab	*Etsī elūē, etsī elōē.*
Merchant	*Shīshōe.*
Mew	*Erōnālā.*
Middling	*Mhōm phiā.*
Middling (as to size)	*Vāntangdrōā.*
Midnight	*Zamō nūngwe, tsangchonūngte.*
Midst	*Ōnūngī.*
Midwife	*Ngāro khīlo ewe, ngāropōko ewe.*
Mighty	*Epvū khyūngwā.*
Mildew	*Phamā.*
Milk, *v.*	*Tshenālā.*
Milk, *n.*	*Shīrōtchhü.*
Milk (clotted)	*Khōnūng.*
Mimic	*Etchu esāntsōālā.*
Mind	*Lamm, lampam.*
Mind (obey)	*Engālā.*
Mine	*Ā.*
Mingle	*Nzütālā, nzütsiālā.*
Mirth	*Emāthā.*
Mirror	*Ōmhā chāmphen.*
Miscarriage	*Etchü pōkā.*
Miserly	*Chīrhrakhāngā.*

Mist . . . *Otchhū etsiro.*
Mist (fog) . . . *Emhentchhü.*
Mistake . . . *Mhechōā.*
Mix . . . *Nzü tsātālā, nzütālā.*
Mixed . . . *Nzütāchākā.*
Moan . . . *Drālā.*
Mock (imitate) . . *Etchü sandryū tsōiyālā, etchü esān tsōālā.*
"Mod" . . . *Sōko.*
"Mod" (strong) . . *Zütsü.*
Modest . . . *Yikrākhangā.*
Moist . . . *Mpōnichākā.*
Moisten . . . *Mpōnyālā.*
Molasses . . . *Nchü shāncho.*
Mole . . . *Yisōpvū.*
Money . . . *Ōtscen, ōrāng.*
Monkey . . . *Khūsho, yāksō.*
Monkey (large) . . *Ōtham.*
Month . . . *Chōro.*
Monthly . . . *Chōro chōro.*
Moon . . . *Chōro.*
Moon (new) . . . *Chōro chōthān.*
Moon (full) . . . *Chōro ekā.*
Moon (waning) . . *Chōro chōyilāmi.*
Moon (time between moons) . . . *Chōram.*
More . . . *Ntangō, ōliwōhā, enōā.*
More . . . *Sā,* (affixed to verb).
Morning . . . *Engyāthang.*
Morning (time of sun rising) *Wōnchiāthang.*
Morning (very early) . *Nyāpā, nyāzāngenā.*
Morrow . . . *Ōchō.*
Mortar (for cleaning *dhān*) *Tsampo, ōtsam.*
Mosquito . . . *Tsokhyū.*
Mother . . . *Ōpvü, aiyō.*
Mother (grand) . . *Ōpvü, ōtsü.*
Mother-in-law . . *Ōno.*
Mould . . . *Phāmālā.*
Mouldy . . . *Phamā.*
Mound . . . *Ephyōng.*
Mount . . . *Chungwālā.*
Mountain . . . *Pūnglān.*

Mountain (range) . .	*Yentsang.*
Mountain (peak) . .	*Pünglāṉ kūrre.*
Mourn . . .	*Nungräthātālā.*
Mouse . . .	*Zirōro.*
Moustache . . .	*Mehm.*
Mouth . . .	*Ōpang.*
Mouth-piece (of a pipe) .	*Ntsapkāpheṉ.*
Move (put in another place).	*Thamphōe vātālā.*
Move (up and down) .	*Enhyōkālā.*
Move (from one residence to another).	*Thamphōe vānai yiālā.*
Move about (restlessly) .	*Nyāphiālā.*
Much . . .	*Elam.*
Mud . . .	*Chōmpyāyū.*
Multitude . . .	*Kyōṉ elam etsci.*
Murder . . .	*Nangthātātālā.*
Murderer . . .	*Langthākhangā.*
Murmur . . .	*Ethōchākāla.*
Murmur (as a stream) .	*Ekhūālā.*
Musical instrument . .	*Khūpheṉ.*
Muskrat . . .	*Teraṉ.*
Mushroom . . .	*Lampheṉ.*
Mustard . . .	*Hāni.*
Musty . . .	*Phamā.*
Mutter . . .	*Pūnyūālā.*
Muzzle . . .	*Emeṉ mānyālā, emeṉ zammiālā.*
Myself . . .	*Āmōmō, āpōpō.*

N

Nail (finger or toe) .	*Yingkyap.*
Nail (carpenter's) . .	*Yōnchāk, eshenkāpheṉ.*
Naked . . .	*Khūso, mpenscü n-khī.*
Name . . .	*Ōmyang.*
Name (call) . . .	*Tsālā.*
Nap, *v.* & *n.* . .	*Echakāro yipālā, terrā yip.*
Nature . . .	*Shentī.*
Narrow . . .	*Kuhrap, zūkhangā.*
Naughty . . .	*Ngāngkhangā.*
Nay . . .	*Me, mak, mek.*
Naval . . .	*Nnā.*

Near (very) . . . *Escapō.*
Near (not far) . . *Enghyāno, nthangō, nkōnkhang.*
Nearly (about) . . *Hākōnō, ekōno.*
Neat . . . *Ntscangā.*
Neck . . . *Engū.*
Neck-cloth . . . *Engūlo ntsakāphen.*
Necklace . . . *Yōko.*
Needle . . . *Ōpyam.*
Needy . . . *Yāntsai, yāntse, ezapthāta.*
Neighbour . . . *Ntangō evān, echauōro, phīnā kī sham.*
Neither, nor . . . *Ha-ha.*
Nephew . . . *Ōngo.*
Nerve . . . *Etho.*
Nerveless . . . *Etho n-chü.*
Nest . . . *Ōshab.*
Net (fish) . . . *Ngōtsōphen.*
Nettle . . . *Sehrā.*
Nettle (large kind) . *Kōkū sehrā.*
Never . . . *Kōthanghā* (with negative).
Nevertheless . . . *Lehā.*
New . . . *Ethan.*
Next . . . *Chyūsilōchū, chisilōchō.*
News . . . *Ōyi*
Nibble . . . *Nkapālā.*
Niece . . . *Ōkā.*
Nice . . . *Tangto mhōnā, elam mhōnā, eze mhōnā.*
Nigh . . . *Enhyāno, escapo.*
Night . . . *Zamōthang, samōlo.*
Night (last) . . . *Nsamō.*
Night (to-night) . . *Ōsamō.*
Night before last . . *Nchō samo.*
Nineteen . . . *Tāro sü-tokū, mekü mentōkū.*
Ninety . . . *Ekhātōkū.*
Nip . . . *Myiro taphrōālā, eyen echaki tsōālā, ntsakālā.*
Nipple . . . *Shiro.*
No . . . *Me, mek, mak.*
No, none . . . *Nyūhā* "*or*" *ntyūhā n ni.*
Nobody . . . *Ōchihā,* (with negative) "*m*" or "*n*".
Nod . . . *Engwālā, engamphiālā.*
Noise (to make) . . *Ngāngwālā, pōrāktālā.*
Noisy . . . *Ngāng.*

Noiseless . . . *Ethang ntsü.*
None (no one) . . *Ōchihā*, (with negative) "*m*" or "*n*."
None (not any) . . *Ntyūhā*, (with negative) "*mak*," "*n-ni*."
Noon . . . *Nshü ethango, engi-onün̲go.*
Noose . . . *Ōzü nkōn̲.*
North . . . *Chüchōwe.*
Nose . . . *Kenno.*
Nose (snout) . . . *Men̲shūng.*
Nostril . . . *Kennōkü.*
Not . . . *N, m.*
Not that . . . *Shi mak, shi mek.*
Not is . . . *N-ti, m-mā, n-chü, n-chi.*
Nothing . . . *Nkyūhā, ntyūhā.*
Not any . . . *Ntyūhā mak, ntyūhā n-ni.*
Notwithstanding . . *Lehā.*
Now . . . *Nthāngā.*
Now-a-days . . . *Epaiyā.*
Number, *v.* . . . *Khālā.*
Numberless . . . *N-khākōk, n-khāche.*
Nurse (ayah) . . . *Ngāro epvwi.*
Nurse, *v.* . . . *Shirōtchhū yūtōkālā, shiro yūtōkālā.*

O

Oar . . . *Ōhrōng ehāphen̲.*
Oath . . . *Echhamā.*
Obey . . . *Ōyi engālā, pangnōcho zōālā.*
Observe (a command) . *Engālā.*
Observe . . . *Zechiā vāmpvü.*
Obstinate . . . *Ryūchākhangā.*
Obstruct . . . *Khānālā.*
Obtain . . . *Yānchetālā, hngchākālā.*
Odour . . . *Ōhram, errā.*
Of . . . *Theni, thangi.*
Lit.—With.
Offence . . . *Phyōphi.*
Offspring . . . *Ōtsōe, ōro, rōro.*
Offering (religious) . . *Emū.*
Often . . . *Nsānsām.*
Oil . . . *Khutchhü, titchhü.*
Older . . . *Erāmō.*

Old (of man or animals)	*Eshōn, erān, sōnchākā.*
Old (of animals or things)	*Ehen, eke.*
Old (very) (of men)	*Hārishiā.*
Old (very) (of things)	*Enhyākā.*
Omnipotent	*N-sündryūkōk nyūhā n-ni.*
On	*Ōpōni,* affixes *o* and *lo.*
Once	*Echūngā, echōā.*
One	*Matsangā, ekhā, ntsangā, nchyüā.*
One hundred	*Nzōā, nzō, ekhātāro*
One (person)	*Nchühā.*
One's self	*Ōmōmō, ōpōpō.*
Onion	*Sāngdrāng.*
Only	Suffix *mōtī, pōtī. ti.*
Only child	*Ōtsōe eponthi.*
Onward (to go)	*Yiā vānālā, wōā vānālā.*
Open (as a box)	*Elhīchiālā.*
Open (as a door)	*Chōnchiālā.*
Open (as eyes)	*Kakātālā.*
Open (as a flower)	*Ekhiālā, ekisōchiālā.*
Open (as the mouth)	*Khūālā.*
Openly	*Ōmpāhngwā.* *Lit.*—In sight of all.
Openly	*Hālāngtō hngwā.*
Or	*Tālo, ālo, osü menā.*
Orange	*Kōngken.*
Order (command)	*Pangnōālā.*
Order, put in	*Nsangi vātālā.*
Ornaments	*Phiphō sampo.*
Orphan	*Ndrü mphen.*
Other	*Thāmphō, ōyām, ōyān, tāmphō,* affix *pōe.*
Our	*E.*
Outside	*Hōmpōwe, hōmphōe, hōnkhwi.*
Outside (end one)	*Ōtānī.*
Overturn	*Khōphiālā, kōpiālā, eyālā.*
Over (above)	*Ōyāki, kurre, lāmhauwe, ōmhauwe.*
Overcome	*Tōālā.*
Overtake	*Pānhyātālā, phānhyātālā.*
Owe	*Epiyū liā, elō liā.*
Owl	*Velangū, venüng.*
Own (one's own)	*Ōmōmō, ōmōchī tsaki.*
Own (possess)	*Liā, vānā.*
Ox	*Māngsü nchotsōncho.*

P

Pace . . . *Khöchiālā.*
Pack . . . *Nkhapcho.*
Paddy . . . *Ōtsök.*
Pain, *v.* . . . *Enöālā.*
Pain, *n.* . . . *Nöā.*
Painful . . . *Nökhangā.*
Paint, *v.* . . . *Rrūchū erānkātālā.*
Pair, (a male and female,) *Ōmpöe, pānipōni.*
Pair (of things) . . *Tsongkhōn̲, tsākai ehān̲.*
Pale . . . *Mipyangpangā.*
Palm (of hand) . . *Myökū.*
Pant . . . *Mhüālā.*
Panther . . . *Tsôngôro.*
Paper . . . *Kāko.*
Parallel . . . *Rentā.*
Pardon . . . *Sī yiālā.*
Pare . . . *Ōfū lammālā, öfū chisiāla.*
Parents . . . *Ōpvū öpö.*
Part . . . *Echü, echi.*
Partition . . . *Drülo.*
Pass (in road) . . *Nkāchitālā.*
Pass (to keep passing) . *Wöyitālā.*
Pat . . . *Thamphiālā.*
Path . . . *Ōlān̲, lāmpöro.*
Patient . . . *Ntsöā.*
"*Pān*" . . . *Ōshāngo.*
Pauper . . . *Yāntse.*
Paw, *v.* . . . *Löko nshākālā.*
Paw (fore) . . . *Ōkhe.*
Paw (hind) . . . *Ōchö.*
Pay . . . *Ōtsen piālā.*
Pay (a debt) . . . *Ōtchī löālā.*
Peace . . . *Mhöntā mhöntsi, nchentā, nkhöntā.*
Peaceful . . . *Mhöntsī changthetā, changtāng, sārang-ā, öhangchangā,*
.Peace-maker . . . *Ōlān̲ elyüe, lān̲yūe.*
Lit.—" A road maker," *öyān ephyo.*
Peak . . . *Kūrre, kūrri.*
Pebble . . . *Nungdrā.*
Peck . . . *Enchiālā.*

Peck . . . *Mphōā chechiālā, mphōāzetāla.*
Peel, *v.* . . . *Ōfū lammālā, ōfū chisiālā, shākisiālā, kokisiālā.*
Peel, *n.* . . . *Sōfū.*
Peg . . . *Eshen thephen.*
Pen . . . *Erāmphen.*
Penis . . . *Ōzang.*
People . . . *Ōyān, ōyām-*
People (of one house) . *Wōpān.*
Pepper . . . *Māchi, māchü.*
Peppery . . . *Tshōā.*
Perch . . . *Eshōnālā.*
Perfect . . . *Tekilā, hinācho m-mhōnkā.*
Perform . . . *Lyūālā.*
Perfume . . . *Ōhram.*
Perhaps . . . *Esā, kōntsyū.*
Perjure . . . *Echang echamālā.*
Perpendicular . . *Ntōng kāchiā.*
Persecute . . . *Ezaptōkālā.*
Person . . . *Nchyūā, ōyān, ōyām.*
Person (another) . . *Ōyām.*
Perspire . . . *Eshāntsangālā, eshāntālā.*
Peruse . . . *Kālā.*
Pestle . . . *Mānki.*
Petty . . . *Echakāro, terraro.*
Phlegm . . . *Enhā, ehno.*
Physic . . . *Ephyo mazzü.*
Physician . . . *Mazz even, rātsen.*
Pice . . . *Poisā, rāngmyo.*
Lit.—Money red.
Pick (as flowers) . . *Hrōnālā.*
Pick (as fruit) . . *Hlōālā.*
Pick (up) . . . *Khiōkātālā.*
Pick (as vegetables) . *Tenālā.*
Picture . . . *Ōmōn lyūcho* (with name of object).
Piece . . . *Echü, echi.*
Pierce . . . *Chenālā, echūngālā, erōkhrapālā.*
Pig . . . *Wōkōro.*
Pig (the call for) . . *Lele lele.*
Pigeon . . . *Tehūrr, vefū.*
Pile, *v.* . . . *Lōlōktscoi vātālā.*
Pile . . . *Khōlōk.*

Pilfer . . .	*Efüālā.*
Pillage . . .	*Shüī khiālā.*
Pillow . . .	*Nkham.*
Pimple . . .	*Shenchecho.*
Pin . . .	*Ōkyo.*
Pinch . . .	*Myāpālā, nphyakī tsangālā.*
Pink, *adj.* . . .	*Drākātā.*
Pipe (tube) . . .	*Yemphen.*
Platform . . .	*Ōsā.*
Play . . .	*Chālātālā, zavātālā, ngāngōtālā.*
Play (a musical instrument).	*Khüālā.*
Please . . .	*Emāthātōkālā.*
Pleased . . .	*Emātsangā.*
Plenty . . .	*Te.*
Pliable (slimsy) . .	*Pīlākā, pīyüā.*
Pluck (as fruit) . .	*Hlōālā.*
Pluck (as leaves) . .	*Tenālā, ntōnālā, lāpālā.*
Plug . . .	*Ndren.*
Plume . . .	*Wōro mhe.*
Pocket . . .	*Scükhü, lamā lamāthephen.*
Pod . . .	*Ōkyab.*
Point . . .	*Myiro.*
Point (to sharpen to a point)	*Nzenālā.*
Point out . . .	*Echüchiālā.*
Poison . . .	*Thryüsā.*
Poison (for killing fish) .	*Ōno.*
Pole . . .	*Ōtsāng tsapō.*
Polish . . .	*Echōālā, ntsālā.*
Pongee . . .	*Ōtscü.*
Pony . . .	*Kürr, korrü.*
Pool . . .	*Tchhükau.*
Poor . . .	*Yāntsai, yāntse, kwürrītsangā.*
Porcupine . . .	*Līso.*
Pork . . .	*Wōrōso.*
Post . . .	*Tehrrü* (middle post of a house), *khimdra.*
Pot . . .	*Ōpfhü.*
Potato . . .	*Hōro.*
Pound, *n.* . . .	*Sīrratālā.*
Pound, *v.* . . .	*Tāpālā.*
Pound (with the fist) .	*Ōkhezamī echüngālā.*

Pound (as *dhán*) . . *Tsiālā, pōtōngtālā, phōnüngtālā* (when two pound together.)
Pounder (*dhán*) . . *Meṉki.*
Pour (in) . . . *Esōkthechiālā.*
Pour (out) . . . *Eshōki shiālā.*
Powerful . . . *Thōngchiā, ethōchiā.*
Practice . . . *Echütālā.*
Praise . . . *Tsai iyālā.*
Pray . . . *Ekhamālā.*
Precede . . . *Ōvangī yiālā.*
Precipice . . . *Kōtsü.*
Pregnant . . . *Ōtsak nchang, ngāro hānā, ōro hānā, ōro chiā.*
Pout, *v.* . . . *Emeṉ ethyüālā, emēṉ ephiātālā.*
Press together . . *Zamiālā, zamālā.*
Pretty . . . *Eze mhōnā.*
Prevent (hinder) . . *Ekhetsiālā, nīyāngtō\kālā.*
Price . . . *Ōmāṉ.*
Present (at hand) . . *Ēpī, hepi, hello.*
Present, *n.* . . . *Ōthāṉ.*
Present, *v.* . . . *Piālā.*
Prick . . . *Erōkālā.*
Pride . . . *Ngāngwā.*
Priest . . . *Emū eyūlo, ewo kyōṉ.*
Prison . . . *Evangkī.*
Profit . . . *Kāk.*
Prohibit . . . *Ekhetsiālā, enīnyāngā.*
Proud . . . *Ngāngkhangā, ngāngwā.*
Puff . . . *Hmtātālā, phūchiālā.*
Puke . . . *Lālā, lātālā.*
Pull . . . *Tsāngālā.*
Pull (up by the roots) . *Rōkālā.*
Pumpkin . . . *Shamō, emyam.*
Punch . . . *Echūngtālā, echūnghrapālā.*
Punish . . . *Ezapālā.*
Pup . . . *Fhūrōro.*
Pupil (of eye) . . *Kākāro, mhyektsang.*
Purchase . . . *Shiālā.*
Purge . . . *Phyōthātālā.*
"Purdah" . . . *Ōscü ki khāṉ pheṉ.*
Pure . . . *Ntsangā.*
Purple . . . *Enyikū.*

Purpose . . . *Lamm.*
Lit.—Mind.

Purse . . . *Ōrāng thephe̱n, rāṉg scü khū.*

Pursue . . . *Phānālā.*

Push . . . *Senchiālā, khiānivāchiālā.*

Push (about, along) . . *Ehālā.*

Put . . . *Vātā, thetā,*

Put (across) . . . *Rōkātālā.*

Put (food in the mouth of another) . . . *Ekhamālā.*

Put in . . . *Eshōālā.*

Put on (as clothes) . . *Mpenālā, sōkthetālā, pokthetāla.*

Put on (as shoes) . . *Shōkhala, hāṉālā.*

Put (wood on fire) . . *Nchakālā.*

Putrid . . . *Kyōnā.*

Q

Quag (mire) . . . *Chōnpyaiyū.*

Quake . . . *Enetālā.*

Quarrel . . . *Pāngtālā, khōntālā.*

Quarter, *adj.* . . . *Pōko tsensōcho.*
Lit.—A divided half.

Quench . . . *Mhetōḳālā, hm mhetālā.*

Quenched (as thirst) . *Erā ekyamchākā.*

Question . . . *Engālā.*

Quick . . . *Setōā, ekhiāpā, ekhyangā, ndrā.*

Quickly . . . *Ekhiōlākā, zākzāk, elāro.*

Quiet (to keep) . . *Yingtōvānālā, ntōvānālā.*

Quietly . . . *Ethak ti tsānā.*
Lit.—Not taking a breath.

Quill . . . *Hm.*

Quite . . . *Echakāro,* (or) *terraro* with a negative.

R

Race, *v.* . . . *Yōngtālā.*

Race, *n.* . . . *Ekūhrū, echüpō.*

Raft . . . *Yaiyim.*

Rafter . . . *Khyūro.*

Rain, *n.* . . . *Erū.*

Rain, *v.* . . .	*Erūchōālā.*
Rainbow . . .	*Sündrākā.*
Rainy . . .	*Erū chōmūngā.*
Rainy season . . .	*Nzüpūngo.*
Raise . . .	*Phichetālā.*
Rake, *v.* . . .	*Khetālā.*
Rake, *n.* . . .	*Hōmphō khephen̲, ōyāk.*
Ram, *n.* . . .	*Kātsō ōpōng, hōlyū ōpōng.*
Ram, *v.* . . .	*Chenālā.*
Ramrod . . .	*Tsangī chemphen̲.*
Rap . . .	*Kōkōkālā.*
Raspberry . . .	*Lekhūkhi.*
Rat . . .	*Ziro.*
Rat (musk) . . .	*Yisōpvū.*
Rattle . . .	*Zāng zāngālā.*
Rattle (in throat) . .	*Threhretālā.*
Ratan . . .	*Rrüpam.*
Ratan (split) . . .	*Ōrrü.*
Ravine . . .	*Ekōke.*
Raw . . .	*M-mhe, eshü.*
Razor . . .	*Ketsilō, kūrrü tsüphen.*
Reach . . .	*Chhānālā.*
Read . . .	*Khālā.*
Ready . . .	*Sālā.*
Real . . .	*Ōtscōtscō.*
Reap . . .	*Ōlidrālā, ntsanālā* (reaping of "koni dhân").
Rear . . .	*Silāmwe, ndrewe.*
Rear (of house) . .	*Khāntsangwe.*
Rebuke . . .	*Pangnōālā.*
Receptacle . . .	*Vāphen̲, thephen̲.*
Recently . . .	*Ōsi.*
Receive . . .	*Hngālā, khiālā.*
Reckon . . .	*Khālā.*
Recognise . . .	*Chethetālā.*
Reconcile . . .	*Ōlān̲ lyūala.* *Lit.*—Make a road.
Recover . . .	*Hngtānālā, yānchenālā.*
Red . . .	*Rākātā, rākhiā, myōnā, myōnshiā.*
Red (colouring matter obtained from the bark of a shrub).	*Lūnghi.*

Red (yarn) . . . *Lănghi.*
Reed . . . *Tsöntsang, pempo.*
Reel . . . *Kōkōn̠, ōying kōnphen̠.*
Reign . . . *Ōmō yitsöālā.*
Reflect . . . *Nchami zetālā.*
Rejoice . . . *Emāthātālā.*
Relative . . . *Pütsō pütso, ekūhrr, wōpān̠.*
Release . . . *Văchiālā.*
Remain . . . *Vānālā.*
Remember . . . *Nchamkātālā, nchamā-vānālā.*
Remove . . . *Thāmpō iyālā.*
Remove (causative) . . *Thāmphō yitōkālā.*
Rengma Nāgā . . *Mōyi, mōyūe.*
Repair . . . *Ethān̠ lyūālā.*
Repeat . . . *Lyūlānālā* (do again).
Repeatedly . . . *Khūki, nsānsām.*
Reply . . . *Yichōālā.*
Report . . . *Ezōālā.*
Report (of a gun) . . *Ekhiwo.*
Reptile . . . *Ndrrü.*
Rescue . . . *Sānchōālā.*
Rescue (from drowning) . *Sachetālā.*
Reside . . . *Vānālā.*
Reside (as a spirit in rocks, &c.) *Mpātālā.*
Resemble . . . *Escā hngā.*
Rest . . . *Mūngālā.*
Restore . . . *Pilānālā.*
Retaliate . . . *Thrālāntālā, thrātālā.*
Return . . . *Elānai iyālā, yilānālā.*
Revenue . . . *Lōkōtsen̠.*
Reward . . . *Ōthān̠.*
Rib . . . *Kyōn̠ ōrrü.*
Rice (paddy) . . . *Ōtsōk.*
Rice (unhulled) . . *Ōtscang.*
Rice (hulled) . . *Ōtsi, ōtsü.*
Rice ("konī dhân") . *Ōten̠.*
Rice ("bora dhân") . *Tsōkpvü.*
Rich . . . *Elī.*
Ride . . . *Māngkwi chūng iyālā.*
Ridge . . . *Hōnki.*
Ridge-pole . . . *Hōnki tsang.*

Rifle . . . *Tsangi.*
Right . . . *Ōtscōtsco.*
Righteous . . . *Ntsōā.*
Right hand . . . *Āmymwe.*
Rim . . . *Ōpang, emen, ōtse, ōtsai.*
Rind . . . *Ōfhū.*
Ring . . . *Yingdrōlo pōktephen.*
Ring (as a bell) . . *Ekhūālā.*
Ripe . . . *Emhe.*
Ripened . . . *Mhenchākā.*
Rise . . . *Pānthiālā.*
Rise (from sleep) . . *Chang iyālā.*
Rise (as a river) . . *Tsülālā.*
River . . . *Pōfū.*
River (other side of) . *Pōfū pānkauwe.*
River (this side of) . . *Pōfū-ōyāmwe.*
Road . . . *Ōlān, pōkilān.*
Roar . . . *Ehrūālā.*
Roast . . . *Phamālā, rrālā.*
Rob . . . *Efūālā.*
Robber . . . *Efūe.*
Rock, *n.* . . . *Nūngpvū.*
Rock, *v.* . . . *Enhyōk phiālā.*
Rod (fishing) . . . *Ōkhūtōng.*
Roll . . . *Erūchiālā, erūphiālā, erai yiālā.*
Roll up . . . *Shüālā.*
Roof . . . *Shüwo.*
Room . . . *Nchen.*
Room (front) . . . *Sōntōyi.*
Room (middle) . . *Thryūhi.*
Room (inner or back) . *Tāchūngwe.*
Roost, *v.* . . . *Khyngālā.*
Roost, *n.* . . . *Hōno khyangphen.*
Root . . . *Ōyang, ōying.*
Root (used for poisoning water in order to procure fish). *Ōno.*
Rope . . . *Ōzü.*
Rot . . . *Kyōnālā, mōrōālā.*
Rotten . . . *Mōrōe sütākā, ekyo kyōndrōā.*
Round . . . *Ekā, mpam.*
Row . . . *Rentā.*

Row (as a boat) . . *Ehākātālā.*
Rub . . . *Mhetālā, mhephiālā.*
Rub (between the hands) . *Nnōkālā.*
Rubber . . . *Ōni.*
Rubber (hard lump of) . *Nitzü.*
Rubber (tree) . . *Ōnitōng.*
Rule . . . *Ōmōyitsōālā, pangnōālà.*
Ruler . . . *Yāntsen etsōe.*
Ruler (rod) . . . *Sephen.*
Run . . . *Escānālā, yūngālā.*
Run against . . . *Chenkātālā, khūkātālā.*
Run away . . . *Tsānālā.*
Run out, as tongue . . *Tsangchetàlā, sechetālā.*
Rupee . . . *Rāmpiāk, ōrāng.*
Rust . . . *Sāsi hyangā.*

S

Sabbath . . . *Emung nchōk.*
Sack . . . *Ōzzü scü.*
Lit.—String cloth.
Sacrifice, *v.* . . . *Emū lyūālā.*
Sacrifice, *n.* . . . *Emū.*
Sad . . . *Nūngrā.*
Saddle, *n.* . . . *Sōfü khōktephen.*
Lit.—Leather seat.
Saddle, *v.* . . . *Sōfü khōktephen erükātālā.*
Safe . . . *Tānangi, rārangi.*
Sahab . . . *Etsi.*
Salary . . . *Ōtsen.*
Saliva . . . *Nchü.*
Salt . . . *Ōmā.*
Saltish . . . *Ōmātav.*
Salute . . . *Khamālā.*
Same . . . *Khiti* (equal), *tsaka chuki.*
Sand . . . *Pōpā.*
Sand fly . . . *Penchakāro.*
Sap . . . *Ōmōtchhü.*
Satisfied . . . *Nhichākā, phyangchākā.*
Save . . . *Vātālā, vālā.*
Save (from drowning) . *Suchetālā.*
Save (from wild beast) . *Sānchōālā.*

Saw, *n*. . . . *Ōtscang thrüphen*.
Saw, *v*. . . . *Thrüālā*.
Say . . . *Phyōālā, ezōālā*.
Scab . . . *Emhokyab, ōmōeyo*.
Scald . . . *Lerōālā, leshākālā*
Scales . . . *Efhū*.
Scallop . . . *Ōren*.
Scalloped . . . *Ōriōren*.
Scalp . . . *Kürrü fhū*.
Scan . . . *Zetālā*.
Scanty . . . *Zānkhangā, zāngkhāngā*.
Scar . . . *Pārāk*.
Scarce . . . *Zānkhangā, zāngkhangā*.
Scatter . . . *Nzesiālā, nrōkālā, tsānsōrōālā*.
Scissors . . . *Oscü nyāphen*.
Scold . . . *Khōnālā, mākālā*.
Scoop, *v*. . . . *Ekhüālā*.
Scoop, *n*. . . . *Mōro*.
Scorch . . . *Tyūng nyikālā*.
Scour . . . *Mhetālā, süālā*.
Scowl . . . *Mhetsang nkapālā*.
Scrape . . . *Sākālā*.
Scratch . . . *Enakālā, nshākālā*.
Scream . . . *Erōnālā*.
Screw . . . *Yōnchāk errücho mmyāthe.. ālā*.
Scrotum . . . *Ncho*.
Seam . . . *Evū, vūcho*.
Search . . . *Yānālā*.
Seat . . . *Khōktephen, evān*.
Secretly . . . *Mphōā*.
Securely . . . *Rārangi*.
See . . . *Mhüngālā, hüngālā ; zetālā*.
Lit.—Look at.
Seed, *n*. . . . *Tsangthi*.
Seed, *v*. . . . *Ethiyālā*.
Seek . . . *Yānālā*.
Seize . . . *Rhamālā, thramātālā*.
Seldom . . . *Kōthangnā kōthangnā, chōcho*.
Select . . . *Zesü khiālā, ekyōe khiālā*.
Self . . . *Ōmōmō, ōpōpō*.
Sell . . . *Yenālā*.
Semen . . . *Zangtchhü*.

English	Lhota
Send away	*Wōtōkālā, yitōkālā.*
Sentry	*Lān̲zām.*
Separate	*Chung chung; champō champō.*
Separately	*Chung chungnā.*
Sepulchre	*Ōlap, ōkhap, ōlab.*
Serpent	*Ndrr.*
Servant	*Chenchi engai.*
Set (place)	*Thetālā, vātālā.*
Set (as the sun)	*Hretālā.*
Set down	*Vātālā.*
Set on fire	*Thyenyala, rongālā.*
Settle	*Nchangālā.*
Seventy	*Ekhātiing.*
Several	*Etham mezza, tārraro.*
Sew	*Vüālā.*
Shade	*Ōmōn̲.*
Shake	*Ennetālā, enghyokālā, ekhyūphiālā.*
Shallow	*Nchōng, pōlā.*
Sham	*Echāng echüphiālā.*
Shame	*Yikrā.*
Share	*Chütālā.*
Share (part)	*Echi.*
Sharp	*Terrterrto, erōā.*
Sharpen	*Ehetālā, phyākālā, nzenālā.*
Shave	*Sākālā, tsiālā.*
She	*Shi.*
Sheath	*Yōndrrü etsānphen̲.*
Sheep	*Kātsō, holyü.*
Shepherd	*Kātsō thrükiwōchü.* *Katsō ekamwōchü.*
Shelf	*Lāmāthanglero vāphen̲, thārāpvūro vāphen̲.*
Shell, *v.*	*Mphakālā.*
Shell	*Chōkō.*
Shell (cowrie)	*Fhufo.*
Shield	*Ōtsōng.*
Shine	*Wōnālā.*
Shining	*Ewōnā.*
Shiver	*Ennetālā.*
Shoe	*Chōkhab.*
Shoot	*Thiālā, khiālā.*
Shop	*Shishōeki.*

Shot . . . *Tsangī tsang.*
Short . . . *Hendruwo, ehngāro, nghangāro, nsükhang.*
Shortly . . . *Esangāro, ōkhānāti, ōkhaicho.*
Shoulder . . . *Epfhū.*
Shoulder, *v.* . . . *Epfhūlo ekātālā.*
Shout . . . *Hōrālā.*
Shove . . . *Sentechiālā, senchiālā, scemphiālā.*
Show . . . *Zetōkālā.*
Shut . . . *Khānālā, hlapālā.*
Shuttle . . . *Tsiro.*
Sick . . . *Rāthātā, pirapthātā, ōtsako ennōmpāpā.*
Side . . . *We, tsātsōkwe.*
Side (front of house) . *Hōmphōwe.*
Side (back of house) . *Khāntsangwe.*
Sieve . . . *Yaiyang, eyingphen.*
Sift . . . *Eyingālā.*
Sigh, *v.* . . . *Ethak tsapō chenālā, emhenālā.*
Sign, *n.* . . . *Chethen.*
Sign, *v.* . . . *Eyōpālā, ōkhe nthang myenālā.*
Sign (one's name) . . *Ōmyang erānālā.*
Silence . . . } *Tangtang khūā.*
Silent . . . }
Silent, to be . . . *Ntō vānālā, yingtō vānālā.*
Silver . . . *Ōrāng.*
Similar . . . *Escātāvā, khitītab, khetitav.*
Sinewy . . . *Ethōkhyangwā.*
Sing . . . *Nyāntālā, elhālā.*
Single . . . *Ōmōti.*
Sink . . . *Chūngthetālā.*
Sip . . . *Mpākphiālā.*
Sister . . . *Ōyūlōe.*
Sister-in-law . . . *Ōmi, ōnshi.*
Sit . . . *Khōkthetālā,*
Sit (by the fire) . . *Ōmi lhāpālā.*
Site . . . *Vāmphen.*
Sitting-place (*a sang*) in the village . . . *Ōscā.*
Sixty . . . *Rōkro.*
Skin, *n.* . . . *Ōfhū.*
Skin, *v.* . . . *Shākālā, shāki shiālā, chisiālā.*
Skull . . . *Mākōk.*

Slack . . . *Tākhyūtōkālā.*
Slanting . . . *Yōphiā.*
Slap . . . *Tamālā.*
Slug . . . *Züsyü.*
Slave . . . *Ndri, ezü* (one purchased).
Slay . . . *Sāthātālā, nangthātālā.*
Sleep . . . *Yipālā.*
Sleepy . . . *Yiphngā, yinghngā.*
Slender . . . *Sōlānterrūwo.*
Slice . . . *Ōpiāk.*
Slightly . . . *Etchükāro.*
Slip . . . *Phyetālā.*
Slippery . . . *Phyephyeto.*
Slit . . . *Thrōnālā, thūsālā, khekālā.*
Sliver . . . *Ōkhyo.*
Slowly . . . *Echamnā, echamchamnā.*
Smack . . . *Ntsapālā.*
Small . . . *Etcakāro, terü, ehngāro, echakchakro.*
Small (fine) . . . *Mānisensenā.*
Small-pox . . . *Nangzāk.*
Smart . . . *Entakālā.*
Smash . . . *Temhrapālā, echōnghrāpālā.*
Smell . . . *Ehnghūālā, engwhālā.*
Smile . . . *Mensetālā.*
Smite . . . *Tamālā.*
Smith . . . *Yōnchōe.*
Smoke, *n.* . . . *Mipōng, ōmi ekhū.*
Smoke, *v.* . . . *Pūngālā.*
Smooth . . . *Phyephyeto, myānā.*
Smother . . . *Emen zamiālā. emen efūiyālā.*
Snail . . . *Züsüv.*
Snake . . . *Ndrrü.*
Snap (the finger) . . *Phyāphyākālā, kāpālā.*
Snatch . . . *Eyāchikhiālā, rechōi khiālā.*
Sneeze . . . *Hātsiālā.*
Snore . . . *Ehretālā, elhōnālā.*
Snuff . . . *Enghūālā.*
Soak . . . *Chamālā, mpōni vātālā.*
Soap . . . *Oscü etsaphen, tasakāphen.*
Sob . . . *Nkiālā.*
Soft . . . *Enyiro, enyipā.*
Softly . . . *Ennāto.*

Soil, *v.*	*Nyenālā.*
Soil, *n*	*Lōko.*
Sole	*Mpho.*
Some	*Terrāro, etchakāro, etham mezza.*
Some one, somebody	*Ōyām, ôchiāṉsānā.*
Something	*Nyūsānā.*
Some time	*Kōthāngsānā.*
Sometimes	*Kōthāngnā kōthāngnā.*
Somewhere	*Kūsānā.*
So much	*Hetātā.*
Son	*Ōtsōe epūe, ōngo.*
Son-in-law	*Ōryūwo.*
Song	*Ōkheṉ.*
Soon	*Nkōm, ōkhānāti.*
Soothe	*Emephiālā.*
Sorcerer	*Rātseṉ.*
Sore	*Emho.*
Sorrow	*Nūngdrā.*
Sorrow, *v.*	*Nūngrālā, nūngrātā.*
Sort, *v.*	*Ekhyūālā.*
Sort, *n.*	*Tuv* (affix).
Soul	*Lampam.*
Sound	*Khūā.*
Sour	*Thenā, thempvūrāngkātā.*
South	*Mphīwe, esānāwe.*
Sow, *n.*	*Wōkō ōkyū.*
Sow (seed)	*Yingālā, ndrōkālā.*
Span	(See Table of Measures).
Spark	*Ōmī ekī.*
Speak	*Phyōlā, nsānālā.*
Spear	*Otsō.*
Spear (ornamented)	*Tāndro.*
Speck	*Ntav, ntūntā.*
Spectacles	*Ewōmpvū, ewōmpheṉ.*
Spherical	*Mpam.*
Spider	*Sānkyō.*
Spider-web	*Pōrak tsūtsū.*
Spill	*Engamchiālā, enhyōk chiālā.*
Spin	*Yenālā.*
Spind'e	*Hmtsū.*
Spirit	*Ōmōṉ.*
Spit	*Nchōkālā.*

Spittle . . . *Nchā.*
Splice . . . *Wövtālā.*
Split . . . *Tsciālā, poktsöālā.*
Spoil . . . *Yüsörāvālā, tsôsörālā.*
Spool . . . *Ōying ndren.*
Spoon . . . *Yengkök.*
Sport, *v.* . . . *Chālātālā, ngāngtālā.*
Spout (water) . . . *Tchhü yencho.*
Spray . . . *Ōtchhü etsero.*
Spread out . . . *Sālā.*
Spread out(to dry) . . *Phikāchiālā.*
Spring, *n.* . . . *Tsangkingthang.*
Spring, *v.* . . . *Enhyōphiyālā.*
Spring (of water) . . *Tchhükhū.*
Sprout . . . *Pōkālā.*
Spy . . . *Ōrririche, örrüeche.*
Square . . . *Tsātsōka, nken meza.*
Squash . . . *Shamō.*
Squeeze . . . *Zūmālā, yetālā.*
Squirrel . . . *Cherhā, taki.*
Stack . . . *Nshan.*
Staff . . . *Chārōng.*
Stag . . . *Sepvü öpōng.*
Stagger . . . *Kemphiālā, ngaphiā iyālā, tsātso tsātsō yiālā.*
Stain, *n.* . . . *Tserakhu mpāpā.*
Stairs . . . *Kōkau, phōpā, pōpā.*
Stamp, *v.* . . . *Echüphyālā.*
Stand up . . . *Pānthiālā.*
Stand still . . . *Mangālā.*
Star . . . *Shāntiwō.*
Stare . . . *Nāng tsāngālā.*
Start out of sleep . . *Yimchang chiālā, yiphyōng chiālā.*
Start (from fear) . . *Tscenai yālā, ekhentōkālā.*
Startle . . . *Echüphiālā, ekhentōkālā.*
Starve . . . *Khāngtsāngālā.*
Stay . . . *Vānālā.*
Steady . . . *Nkālā, renchākā,c hang-changto.*
Steal . . . *Efüālā.*
Steal away . . . *Mpōā tsānālā, mphōā tsānālā.*
Steam . . . *Etak.*
Steep . . . *Ekhūā, lānti, chenkhū.*

Stem . . . *Ōkhi.*
Stem (pipe) . . . *Kāpen, kāphen, ntsāp kāphen.*
Stench . . . *Nānā.*
Step . . . *Kōchiā.*
Step (of a ladder) . . *Khōrā, khōkhān, pōphā.*
Sterile . . . *Hāchāng.*
Stern (of a boat) . . *Emen.*
Stick . . . *Ōtscang.*
Stick in . . . *Echong ki vātālā, erōki vātālā.*
Stick in (as a spear in the ground) . . . *Lenālā.*
Stick together . . *Zapkātālā.*
Stick, walking . . *Chārōng.*
Stiff . . . *Khyōngterōkā.*
Still . . . *Tangtangkhūā, yingtō, ntō.*
Sting, *n.* . . . *Khū.*
Sting, *v.* . . . *Takālā.*
Stink . . . *Nānālā, nnā shō shōkālā, nnanchākā, ōhramnā ōyi evakā.*
Stir . . . *Ehāphiālā shūng phiālā, thrōphiālā.*
Stitch . . . *Evü.*
Stone . . . *Ōlūng, ōnūng.*
Stone, god of . . . *Tsangdhrām.*
Stoop . . . *Nkham thetālā, nkhū thetālā.*
Stop . . . *Ōsā, vānālā.*
Stopper . . . *Ndren.*
Storm . . . *Tsōngrōmphen.*
Stout . . . *Epvū khyūngwā, etho khyūngwā.*
Straight . . . *Nsā, sāksākto.*
Straighten . . . *Nsā lyūālā.*
Strain . . . *Tsangālā.*
Strain (filter) . . *Rōnālā.*
Stranger . . . *Kyōn, ethān.*
Lit.—New man.
Kyōn thāmphō.
Lit.—Another man.
Straw . . . *Mōthōng, mavü.*
Stream . . . *Zükhūrō.*
Strength . . . *Ethō, epvwi.*
Stretch . . . *Tsangtālā, rangpūsiālā.*
Strike . . . *Tamālā, tāpālā.*
Strike (as a gong) . . *Ekhōphiālā.*

String . . .	*Oiyang, ozzü.*
Stockade . . .	*Epi.*
Stomach . . .	*Mmā.*
Stumble . . .	*Nshiālā, nshi ekhangālā.*
Submerge . . .	*Changthetālā, changtetālā.*
Subside (as a swelling) .	*Supātā.*
Subside (as a storm) .	*Pochai yālā.*
Substitute . . .	*Thōng.*
Succeed (as one generation succeeds another) .	*Rentālā.*
Succession . . .	*Chūngtā.*
Such . . .	*Hetūv, chitūv.*
Suck . . .	*Ntsapālā.*
Suffice . . .	*Tetsōālā.*
Sugar-cane . . .	*Tsangtchhü nchü.*
Suicide . . .	*Eyen mōntsōi chiā.*
Summer . . .	*Nzütsotsōlō.*
Summon . . .	*Tsālā.*
Sun . . .	*Eng, engi.*
Sunlight . . .	*Engi tāngtāngto.*
Sunrise . . .	*Eng chirōāthang.*
Sunset . . .	*Engi thretathang.*
Support (hold up) . .	*Ekhyōnālā, nkhan ziālā.*
Support (maintain) . .	*Süphiālā, süphi chetālā.*
Supreme . . .	*Tsapōwō, shiyi.*
Surely . . .	*Ōtscōtscō.*
Surround . . .	*Ekōnālā, hālā.*
Suspend . . .	*Hōksi vātālā.*
Swallow, *n.* . . .	*Tsōng ngōro.*
Swallow, *v.* . . .	*Nzü thetālā, nzālā*
Swamp . . .	*Lōko ndrān.*
Swear . . .	*Echamtālā.*
Sweat, *n.* . . .	*Eshāngtchhü.*
Sweat, *v.* . . .	*Eshāng tsangālā.*
Sweep . . .	*Khetālā.*
Sweet . . .	*Nangā.*
Sweetheart . . .	*Ōshamm, eyingā khangdrōe.*
Swell . . .	*Pamālā.*
Swim . . .	*Ōtchhü hüālā, hōkātālā.*
Sword . . .	*Yōndrrü.*
Swing . . .	*Yaiyimālā.*

T

Table . . .	*Pilang.*
Tadpole . . .	*Ngōkhūwo, ngōlāntiwo.*
Tail . . .	*emhi, emhen.*
Tail feather . . .	*Eli, eyū, emhen.*
Tailor . . .	*Ōscü eve.*
Take . . .	*Khiālā, penālā.*
Take and come (bring) .	*Hānsi iyālā, hānsi rōālā.*
Take and go (take away)	*Hānsi iyālā, hanse wōālā, sōsi yiālā, sōsi wōālā.*
Take out . . .	*Khichetālā, chichetālā, hōmphōe chi yitōkā.*
Take up . . .	*Khikātālā.*
Take (with the finger and thumb) . . .	*Ntseni khiālā.*
Take (between the fingers)	*Nghen penālā, nghāiyipenāla nghen khiālā.*
Take off . . .	*Elhichōālā, khichōālā.*
Take on (as clothing) .	*Ephe chiāllā.*
Take one's part . .	*Themō thetālā.*
Take care of . . .	*Scüphiālā, tānangālā, zetā vānalā.*
Talk . . .	*Chāntālā.*
Tall . . .	*Ephiā, thangchu kerāngā, saphō.*
Tally . . .	*Lekham vātālā.*
Tame . . .	*Ezsā.*
Tank . . .	*Wüzü.*
Taste . . .	*Tsōpi zetālā.*
Tax . . .	*Lōko tsen, okitsen.*
Tax-gatherer . . .	*Lōko tsen ekhi.*
Tax-payer . . .	*Lōko tsen ekhe, lōkotsen epi.*
Tea . . .	*Lōmo sōko.*
Tear, *n.* . . .	*Esütchhü.*
Tear, *v.* . . .	*Resōālā, rerūālā, phirōālā, nkhū rōalā, nshū rōālā.*
Tear up (by roots) . .	*Rōkālā.*
Tear (with teeth) . .	*Nkōkālā, nkakālā.*
Teat . . .	*Ntsaphen, ntsap kāphen.*
Teeth . . .	*Ōho.*
Teeth (front) . . .	*Ōho tōnthryūlo.*
Teeth (back) . . .	*Hokōng.*

Teething . . . *Ōḥo shūngā.*
Tell . . . *Ezōālā.*
Tempest . . . *Tsangrōngphen, rruchangkūnyā.*
Ten . . . *Tāro, terro.*
Tend . . . *Tanangālā, sōsu mungālā.*
Tender . . . *Enyipā.*
Tent . . . *Scüki.*
Lit.—(Cloth house).
Terrified . . . *Ekhen tsangā, ekhyū tsangā.*
Test . . . *Mhōmhōnānā zetalā.*
Testicle . . . *Nchotscang.*
Than . . . *Wō.*
That . . . *Ōchi, chi.*
Thatch . . . *Leshü.*
"Thebzothu" . . *Tuyū enūng, tiyi enūng.*
Theft . . . *Efüā.*
Then . . . *Chithang.*
There . . . *Ōchi.*
Thereafter . . . *Chüsicho.*
Therefore . . . *Chitsakōnā, chülōnā, chitōlüi.*
Thereupon . . . *Tōlüisi, chitōlüisi.*
They . . . *Shiāng, shiāno, ōteno, ōnno chiāng, chiāno.*
They (all) . . . *Ōten, ōnten mpān, ōmpā.*
Thick . . . *Chhia, chilo kāngkangā, nkhangā.*
Thigh . . . *Kāngken.*
Thief . . . *Efüe, efwi.*
Thieve . . . *Efüālā.*
Thin . . . *Epiākā, epōrōā, kürrtsangā, wōshākā.*
Thing . . . *Thārāphüro, ōlānthāro* (everything).
Think . . . *Nchamālā, nchami zetālā.*
Third . . . *Ōvangochi tō ōni silāmo.*
Third (day after) . . *Zamchö, ōchö nnang.*
Thirsty . . . *Erātsangā, erāthātā.*
Thirteen . . . *Tāro sü etham.*
Thirty . . . *Thamdro.*
This . . . *Shi, hi.*
This, that . . . *Shi, chi.*
This and that . . *Lāmā lāmā, lāmātero, lāmāthangterro.*
Thorn . . . *Ōkyo.*
Thousand . . . *Thāngā, nzō nzō tavtero.*
Thrash . . . *Ōli tsenālā.*
Thread . . . *Ōying.*

Three . . .	*Etham.*
Thrice . . .	*Chōtham.*
Throat . . .	*Yingkhiro.*
Throw away . . .	*Siālā.*
Throw (hurl) . . .	*Scamchiālā.*
Throw into . . .	*Vātechiālā, shamtechiālā.*
Throw over the shoulder .	*Mpenālā.*
Throw against . .	*Ephiākātālā, shangkātālā.*
Thumb . . .	*Yingpvū.*
Thunder, *v* . . .	*Echēnālā.*
Thus . . .	*Hetō.*
Tick (as a watch) . .	*Tsāk tsāk khūmōngālā, tsāk tsākālā.*
Tickle . . .	*Ezakālā.*
Tie . . .	*Ntsiālā.*
Tie together . . .	*Ntscütscütālā, chüng thryüālā, chüng-tsālā.*
Tiger . . .	*Mharr.*
Tight . . .	*Thangthangto.*
Tightly . . .	*Rārangi, rakrak, tānangā.*
Tigress . . .	*Mharr ōkhö.*
Time . . .	*Thang.*
Timid . . .	*Kūthātā, ekutsangā.*
Tin . . .	*Yōnchāk, yōngchāk.*
Tipsy . . .	*Kinōā.*
Tired . . .	*Mōkthātā, mōktsangā.*
Toad . . .	*Chākū.*
Toad-stool . . .	*Lamphen.*
Tobacco . . .	*Mekhū.*
Tobacco pipe . . .	*Mekhū kūtōng.*
To-day . . .	*Nching.*
Toe . . .	*Chōyingdro.*
Toe-nail . . .	*Chōying kyap.*
Together . . .	*Nzo, nzo ramto.*
Together, to place, *v.* .	*Tsōtsi vātālā, tsōtsenālā, khōlōk tsōi vātālā, nshātscōālā.*
Toil . . .	*Nsündrū, elapā, ehiā.*
To-morrow . . .	*Ōchö.*
To-morrow (day after) .	*Rāchö.*
To-morrow (day after day after).	*Zamchö.*
Tongue . . .	*Nni, nli.*
To-night . . .	*Ōsammo, nching sammō.*

Too	*Hā.*
Tool	*Nsündrüpheṉ.*
Tooth	*Ōho.*
Tooth (front)	*Ōhotonhrülo.*
Tooth (double)	*Hokōng.*
Top (on)	*Ōpōnī.*
Top, *n.*	*Kurre, myiro, phiro.*
Top (of head where the hair is uncut).	*Chāng chāng.*
Torch	*Milōṉ.*
Tortoise	*Shufhū.*
Total	*Ōmpā.*
Touch	*Epyāmphiālā, tsamphiālā, sukātālā.*
Towards	*Ethenī, ethangi.*
Towards	Affix *we.*
Track	*Ōsü, khōsü.*
Trade (exchange)	*Thōngtālā.*
Trade	*Shīshōālā, otseṉ tsōālā.*
Transfix	*Khāntrā echūngālā.*
Transplant	*Chamālā.*
Trap, *n.*	*Vakshub, ōkyō.*
Travel	*Khyaiyālā. sāmphiā wōālā.*
Tread on	*Hnyetālā.*
Tree	*Ōtōng.*
Tree (fruit)	*Tsangthī tōng.*
Tremble	*Ennetālā, ekhūthātālā.*
Trench	*Zükhūrå.*
Tribe	*Kuhrr.*
Trip	*Shiye ekhangālā.*
Trouble	*Emmōkā.*
Trigger	*Kārā, shīpheṉ.*
Trunk of tree	*Tōngpvü.*
Truth	*Nsāyi.* *Lit.*—Straight words. *Ōtscōtscō.*
Truthful	*Nsā.*
Truly	*Ōtscōtscō.*
Tub (for liquor)	*Sōkōcheṉ.*
Tub (bath-tub)	*Tsākāpheṉ.*
Tube	*Ōtchhü yempheṉ, tchhūkhi.*
Tumble	*Yāngphiālā, nkānūng sōrāvālā.*
Turban	*Kūrrilo eyikāpheṉ.*

Turn out . . . *Mmilānālā.*
Turn back . . . *Elānai iyālā.*
Turn over . . . *Khōphiālā, edrālā khōā iyālā.*
Turn round . . . *Nyā phiālā.*
Turn round . . . *Hāri phiālā.*
Turn upside down . . *Chenkhūwo vātālā.*
Turns (by) . . . *Nnītā, chūngtā.*
Tusk . . . *Ōho.*
Twenty . . . *Mekü, mekwi.*
Twice . . . *Chōnī, echūngenni.*
Twin . . . *Nsamtso.*
Twine . . . *Ōzzü.*
Twine (around) . . *Yōkātālā.*
Twist . . . *Nyātālā, erālā.*
Two . . . *Eni, ōnī.*

U

Udder . . . *Shuropang.*
Ugly . . . *Eze m-mhō.*
Umbrella . . . *Phüchōwō.*
Unable . . . *Ntō, nkhyō, n-kōk, n-che.*
Unarmed . . . *Pheshu.*
Unbearable . . . *Elāntsangā.*
Unbenevolent . . . *Tchurākhangā.*
Unbidden . . . *Ntsāhā.*
Unbind . . . *Ephechiālā, lāmpetālā.*
Unbutton . . . *Ephe chiālā.*
Uncertain . . . *Ōtōngōchü ntso.*
Uncertain . . . (See perhaps).
Uncle (paternal) . . *Āpōrāmō, ōpōro.*
Uncle (maternal) . . *Ōphyo.*
Unclean . . . *Myenā.*
Uncork . . . *Tsang chetālā, phechetālā.*
Uncooked . . . *Eshu.*
Unconscious . . . *Zanghā.*
Uncover . . . *Khīkātālā.*
Under . . . . *Ōkapi, ōkhapi.*
Underneath . . . *Ōkapwe, ōkhapwe.*
Understand . . . *Ntsīālā.*
Undress . . . *Ōscü pōkchetāla, ephechiālā.*
Undulating . . . *Kōchu kōrā.*

Unequal . . . *Khiti mak, m-myāntā; sapō hendryū*
Lit—Long and short.
Tsapo terū.
Lit—Large and small.
Uneven . . . *Kōkhūkōrā, m-myā.*
Unfasten . . . *Ephe chiālā, lāmphetālā.*
Unfertile . . . *Hāchāng.*
Unfold . . . *Ekhi lānālā, ephe chiālā.*
Unhappy . . . *Tsang kavhānkab khangā.*
Unhealthy . . . *Ōtsako emū mpankhangā.*
Uninhabited . . . *M-māṉ.*
Unite . . . *Wōtālā, chüngtālā.*
Unkind . . . *N-zāṉ, hārōkhangā, verōkā.*
Until . . . *Ephe chiālā, tāmphetālā.*
Until . . . Expressed by negative participial forms in *thang*, e.g., *n-yithang* until one comes.
Untrue . . . *Echang, n-tsa, ōtscōtscō mak.*
Untwist . . . *Ekhi lāṉālā.*
Unripe . . . *M-mhe.*
Unroll . . . *Lānsō chiālā, ephe chiālā, ekhilānālā.*
Unsteady . . . *Kālāpā.*
Up . . . *Chūng* (prefixed to verb "go" or "come.")
Upper . . . *Ōmhai, ōpōmwe.*
Upon . . . *Ōpōṉi.*
Upon . . . *Lo* (suffixed to nouns).
Upper . . . *Lānghāwōchü.*
Upright . . . *Ntōngkātā.*
Upset . . . *Kāchō chiālā.*
Upward . . . *Ōmhāuwe.*
Urinate . . . *Myongālā.*
Urine . . . *Myongtchhü.*
Use . . . *Ethe lyūālā.*
Useful . . . *Ethe yiā, ethe liā.*
Useless . . . *Ntülāhā m-pāng, nyūla m-pāng, ethe n-ṉi.*

V

Vacant . . . *Echang.*
Vagina . . . *Oshü.*
Vain (useless) . . . *Ntü lihā mpānq.*

Vain . . . *Ngāng khangā, ōyān chāllā khangā.*
Valley . . . *Ekōk.*
Valuable . . . *Ōmā elam, tangtotsakā.*
Vapour . . . *Ethak.*
Variety . . . *Pyōnpo, thāmphō.*
Veal . . . *Māngsürōso.*
Vegetable . . . *Ōhāṉ.*
Vein . . . *Ethō.*
Vend . . . *Yenālā.*
Venom . . . *Ōno, etchhu massü.*
Verandah . . . *Kipang.*
Verdant . . . *Nyāk zangā.*
Very . . . *Mpemō, tangto.*
Very far . . . *Ekōni, elam kōnā, tangto kōnā.*
Vex . . . *Khāng shiālā.*
Victor . . . *Tōā.*
Victorious . . . *Ōyān tōkhangā.*
Victuals . . . *Etsōyü.*
Vigilant . . . *Chetang mātangā, mhyek-rānā.*
Vigorous . . . *Etho khyüngwā, epvü khyüngwā.*
Vehicle . . . *Zōtō.*
Village . . . *Ōyāṉ.*
Village chief . . . *Ekhang wōchü.*
Vine . . . *Ōsü.*
Virgin . . . *Lōrōe.*
Visage . . . *Ōmhā.*
Voice . . . *Ōwō.*
Vomit . . . *Lātālā, lāvsālā.*
Vulture . . . *Mangtso.*

W

Wag . . . *Eye phiālā.*
Wages . . . *Ōtseṉ.*
Wagon . . . *Zōtō.*
Wag tail . . . *Pōtsü sāngsu, rāme siro.*
Waist . . . *Erü.*
Waist-band . . . *Erülo tsāk tepheṉ.*
Wait . . . *Ōsā, vānā.*
Wait for . . . *Nhyākā vānālā.*
Wait upon . . . *Chenchü engālā.*

Wake, *v.* . . .	*Yiptang chiālā, yimon chiālā.*
Wake (another) . .	*Ntechiālā.*
Walk . . .	*Sāmphiā iyālā, thöng phiā yiālā, sephiā iyālā, khai iyālā.*
Walk (pace) . . .	*Khöchiālā.*
Walking-stick . .	*Chārōng.*
Wall (stone) . . .	*Ōnūng ephi.*
Wall (of house) . .	*Echūng.*
Wane (as moon) . .	*Zakātā yiālā.*
Want . . .	*Chōnālā, hngālā, tscōālā.*
War, *v.* . . .	*Ōrrü tsōtālā.*
Warm . . .	*Elamā, lamā, emhākā, ephiā, tscōā.*
Wash . . .	*Epyhōpālā.*
Wash (clothes) . .	*Etsiālā.*
Wash (dishes) . .	*Süālā.*
Wash (face) . . .	*Myüālā.*
Wash (feet) . . .	*Phiālā.*
Wash (hands) . .	*Ntsakālā.*
Wasp . . .	*Chenkōkū, tsipuro.*
Waste . . .	*Yūsōrā chākālā.*
Watch, *v.* . . .	*Hnyākālā, setālā.*
Watch, *n.* . . .	*Ōsen.*
Water . . .	*Ōtchhü.*
Water, to draw . .	*Rānālā*
Water-fall . . .	*Netang.*
Water-fowl . . .	*Tchhü wōro.*
Water-god . . .	*Sangdhrāmm.*
Wave (as water) . .	*Epākātālā, enhyokphiālā.*
Wave (as a flag) . .	*Ehraphiālā, ehraphitālā.*
Waver . . .	*Ngāphiā tsātālā, tsātsō tsātālā.*
Waver (in mind) . .	*Wō yi wō lān tsōālā.*
Wavering . . .	*Shamdrō shamtsiā.*
Wax (ear-wax) . .	*Enno tchhü.*
Wax (bees-wax) . .	*Erān, erā.*
Wax (vegetable) . .	*Ōtōng tsütse.*
Way (road) . . .	*Ōlān, pōkilā* (high-way).
We . . .	*E, enā, ete.*
Weak . . .	*Etho n-chü.*
Wealthy . . .	*Eli, eyi.*
Wear (earrings) . .	*Ennōālā.*
Wear (bracelet) . .	*Penālā.*
Wear (necklace) . .	*Eyikālā.*

Wear (clothes) . . . *Mpenālā.*
Wear (shoes, kilt) . . *Pōkthetālā, hānālā.*
Wear (hat) . . . *Khōālā.*
Weary . . . *Emhōkthātā.*
Weather . . . *Tsanglā.*
Weave . . . *Takālā.*
Web, spider . . . *Pōrāk tsütsü.*
Wed . . . *Sōāvānālā.*
Weed . . . *Lōmō.*
Week . . . *Tsangōtsung, nchōk tsung.*
Weep . . . *Kiāpālā, kiālā.*
Weigh . . . *Fūālā.*
Weight . . . *Efū.*
Well (in body) . . *Pōā, enyipā.*
Well, *n.* . . . *Tchhü kau.*
Well, *adv.* . . . *Mhōnā.*
West . . . *Eng ehrelāmwe.*
Lit.—Direction of sun's *setting.*
Eng hrephemwe.
Wet . . . *Nchiā.*
What . . . *Ntiō, ntyū.*
Wheel . . . *Eriphipheṉ.*
When . . . *Kōthang.*
When, then . . . *Kōthang-ĉhīthang.*
Whence . . . *Küinā, kūlōnā.*
Where . . . *Kūlō.*
Where, there . . *Kūwe-chi.*
Whet . . . *Ehetālā, piākālā.*
Whetstone . . . *Mōrāk, lepōk piākpheṉ, lepōk eheṉpheṉ.*
Which . . . *Ōchō.*
Which . . . *Kūwe, kū.*
While . . . *Thang.*
Whirl . . . *Emungālā, hāralā, hārüphiālā.*
Whiskers . . . *Khōkā hm.*
Whisper, *v.* . . . *Mpōā chāntālā, mphōā chāntālā.*
Whisper, *v.* . . . *Ōkapinā chāntālā.*
Whistle, *v.* . . . *Sükheṉ khūālā.*
White . . . *Emhūā.*
White (very) . . . *Emhūā rōrōā.*
White-ant . . . *Nkhiā.*
Whitish . . . *Etchakāro emhūā, emhūrōā.*
Whither . . . *Kūi, kuwe.*

Whittle . . . *Nsenālā.*
Who . . . *Ōchō, ōchōnā.*
Whoever . . . *Ōchihā, ōchō-chi, ōchōsānā.*
Whole . . . *Ntsōng, ekāni, sāni.*
Whole . . . *Tsu* affixed to nouns.
Whose . . . *Ōchō.*
Why . . . *Ntsōle, nyūwōtsōle.*
Wicked . . . *Hārōkā, verōkā.*
Wide . . . *Nzōā, kōtsā.*
Widen . . . *Nzōā lyūālā, kōtsā lyūā.*
Widow . . . *Emi.*
Widower . . . *Khyingdran̲.*
Wife . . . *Ōki khamm.*
Wife . . . *E-ng, engū. ōki khamm.*
Wife (first) . . . *Lohen̲.*
Wife (new, second) . . *Lothān̲.*
Wild . . . *Ndrākā.*
Wild animal . . . *Ōrā sōngo.*
Wild cat . . . *Tsungōro.*
Will . . . Affix *kā* and *ke.*
Wind (air) . . . *Zūrro.*
Wind . . . *Mpōng, tsangrōngphhen̲* (strong wind).
Wind . . . *Rrūchāngkūnyan* (very strong wind).
Wind up . . . *Nyāphiālā.*
Wind-pipe . . . *Ekhiing, kḥiro.*
Wing . . . *Echo.*
Wink . . . *Ekyāpālā.*
Winnow . . . *Zānālā.*
Winter . . . *Etsako.*
Wipe . . . *Mhetālā.*
Wise . . . *Ntsū, ntsiā.*
Wish . . . *Chōnālā, hngālā.*
With . . . *Nā* (suffixed to nouns).
With . . . *Pānā, phānā, nzo, sūrra, sōsi.*
Within . . . *Tāchūngwe, ōchūngwe.*
Without . . . *Hōmpōe, hōmphōwe.*
Without . . . By negative participle, *e.g.*, Can't go without eating = *n̲-tsōnā ānā n-wōkōk.*
Witness . . . *Ehngwi.*
Wokha (vicinity of) . . *Ndrangi.*
Woman . . . *Elūē, elūe, elōe.*
Woman (young) . . *Lōrūe, lōrōe.*

Womb . . . *Ngāro hāmpen, ngāro hāmphen.*
Wonder . . . *Emhōkālā.*
Wonderful . . . *Emhōktātā, emhōkthātā.*
Wood . . . *Ōtscang.*
Wood, bundle of . . *Tscangpāmpōng.*
Wood (fire-wood) . . *Ōtscang nchakū.*
Wood (forest) . . *Enūng.*
Wood, pile of . . . *Tscangpāmpōng, tscammāntang.*
Wool . . . *Ōtscān, ōhm.*
Word . . . *Ōyī.*
Work, *v.* . . . *Nsūndrālā, elapālā.*
Work, *n.* . . . *Nsündrü.*
Work (house-work) . *Ōkilo ehiā.*
World . . . *Līmhātsū, līmhātshū.*
Worm . . . *Chālyū, ōrā.*
Worship . . . *Khamālā.*
Wound, *v.* . . . *Nanghrapīālā.*
Wound, *n.* . . . *Pārāk.*
Wrap, *v.* . . . *Eyōkālā, nkapālā.*
Wriggle . . . *Nkānphīālā, süphīālā, nyāphiālā.*
Wrist . . . *Khemhyek.*
Write . . . *Erānālā.*
Writing . . . *Erāmo.*
Wrong, to do . . . *Yūsōrātālā, m-mhōm lyūālā.*
Wrong . . . *M-mhō.*
Wrongly . . . *Silyūwo, m-mhōm.*

Y

Yard . . . *Kimang.*
Yard (in length) . . *Khechü enni.*
Yard, *v.* . . . *Ki mango ekam techiālā.*
Yarn . . . *Nünghe.*
Yawn . . . *Hōmhüālā.*
Ye . . . (See "*You.*")
Year . . . *Nzüā.*
Yearly . . . *Nzü nzü.*
Yelk . . . *Ōngā.*
Yell . . . *Hōrālā, nzākālā.*
Yellow . . . *Hākhuā.*
Yes . . . *Ho, hōkhā, hm.*
Yesterday . . . *Nchö.*

Yesterday (day before)	*Ōrāṉ.*
Yet	*Nthāngā.*
Yolk	*Ōngā.*
Yonder	*Ōchi, ōchiche.*
You, *sing.*	*Nō, nnō, nnā.*
You, *plur.*	*Ninō, nte.*
You two, you three	*Nīni, nintham.*
Young	*Khyangdrōe.*
Younger	*Nungōwo.*
Youngest	*Ōkhauwo.*
Yours	*Ni.*
Yourself	*Nimōmō.*
Youth	*Khyangrōthang.*

Z

Zealous	*Lamm khyngā.*

Government of India Central Printing Office.—No. 2 S. to C. C. Assam.—8-3-88.—450.